The Art of the
SMOOTHIE BOWL

Beautiful Fruit Blends for
Satisfying Meals and Healthy Snacks

NICOLE GAFFNEY
Founder of Soulberri Smoothies and Bowls

PAGE STREET
PUBLISHING CO.

PAGE STREET
PUBLISHING CO.

First published in 2019 by
Page Street Publishing Co.
27 Congress Street, Suite 105
Salem, MA 01970
www.pagestreetpublishing.com

Distributed by Macmillan, sales in Canada by The Canadian Manda Group.

23   22   21   20   19   1   2   3   4   5

ISBN-13: 978-1-62414-701-2
ISBN-10: 1-62414-701-1

Library of Congress Control Number: 2018958760

Cover and book design by Rosie Stewart for Page Street Publishing Co.
Photography by Nicole Gaffney

Printed and bound in China

DEDICATED TO MY LATE MOTHER,
GRACE, WHO PASSED DOWN HER LOVE
OF READING, WRITING AND, MOST
IMPORTANTLY, EATING.

◀ ◢ ▶

Contents

◀▲▶

WE ALL SCREAM FOR NICE CREAM — 107

TOPPINGS ARE EVERYTHING — 139

Introduction

My history with making smoothies dates back all the way to when I was fourteen years old and had my very first summer job. It was at a little shop called California Fruit Shake and Yogurt Company, and we sold fresh-fruit smoothies, aka "fruit shakes," which were a relatively new concept on the East Coast at the time. It wasn't long before smoothies absolutely blew up on the scene and everyone and their mothers started drinking them. Fast forward twenty years, and smoothies are still trending in a big way. But why?

The answer is easy. Smoothies are a delicious way to drink all sorts of nutrients. The fact that you can cram so many superfoods into a thick beverage that tastes like a milkshake is enough to explain how this trend actually keeps growing. Now, I'm seeing the focus shift more and more to smoothie bowls, and I think it's because they're just more interesting to eat—not to mention their gorgeous appearance makes them far more photo-worthy and all the rage on social media.

Drinking your meals can get boring; just ask anyone who's ever had to have their jaw wired shut. People want the satisfaction that comes with the feeling of actually eating something rather than sipping it through a straw, and the act of chewing goes a long way in doing that. Smoothie bowls boast the

same flavor profiles, the same nutrition and the same cooling effect as smoothies, but with the added value of texture. As a chef, texture is extremely important to me, and that's why smoothie bowls have completely won my heart.

I had my first ever smoothie bowl on a surf vacation in Rincon, Puerto Rico in 2013. It was an açaí bowl, and at the time I'd never heard of them before. I'll never forget taking my first bite while sitting poolside with my legs dangling in the water. I was blown away by the variation of flavors, but even more so, by the textures. The frosty frozen açaí base was sweet, refreshing and studded with different pieces of dried and fresh fruit, crunchy granola, smooth swirls of peanut butter and hardened bits of coconut oil that melted the second they hit your tongue. It was the ideal treat to eat in the morning before heading out to surf and an even better way to refuel after a long hot day in the sun. I was hooked.

Not long after that experience, I started seeing açaí bowls everywhere. Shops started popping up around the area, and artfully designed bowls began flooding my Instagram feed. Next thing I knew it was pitaya bowls, then green bowls, then smoothie bowls in just about any flavor you can imagine. I saw the trend starting to snowball, and it was clear that just like smoothies, smoothie bowls were not going anywhere.

In 2017 I opened Soulberri Smoothies and Bowls in my hometown of Brigantine, New Jersey, along with my husband, Chaser, and our partner, Will. It was a welcome addition to our sleepy little beach town and has since become a local institution. We operate out of a converted shipping container, which is a pretty tight space, so we keep our menu short and sweet in the name of functionality. Our menu is comprised of several different smoothies and four distinct types of fully customizable smoothie bowls: açaí, green, tropical and nice cream. While the smoothies are certainly popular, we've become known for these smoothie bowls, or "Soul Bowls" as we call them.

While smoothie bowls may seem like they're merely smoothies served in a bowl with some toppings, they actually differ mainly in consistency. While a smoothie has to be thin enough to sip, a smoothie bowl takes on a texture closer to ice cream. The blended fruit in a smoothie bowl is meant to be thicker than a smoothie so that the toppings become suspended and you can scoop up the mixture with a spoon. Any smoothie can become a smoothie bowl and vice versa simply by adjusting the amount of liquid and either adding or removing toppings, but making a proper smoothie bowl requires just a bit more know-how.

The bowls in this book range from the Classic Açaí (page 13) and other crowd-pleasing basics, to adventurous bowls that are a bit more unusual, like the Thai Mango Peanut (page 22). In addition, you'll find all of the little tricks and techniques I've learned and developed over the years to create beautiful, thick and creamy smoothie bowls every single time. There truly is an art to making a great smoothie bowl, both in flavor and appearance, and this book is intended to not only provide you with exciting and unique recipes to follow, but also to give you the knowledge and tools necessary for becoming a master of the craft.

Today, it feels like my life has come full circle. With a smoothie bowl shop under my belt, and now a smoothie bowl cookbook, it's almost as if my fourteen-year-old self was foreshadowing my life to come. I'm thrilled to share these recipes, which include many of our Soulberri staples. Some people were shocked when I told them I'd be including our signature recipes in this book, but I've never believed in keeping recipes a secret.

Smoothie bowls are one of the best ways I know to get people to incorporate more fresh fruits and vegetables into their diets without feeling deprived of flavor and satisfaction. I believe that by sharing the recipes I worked so hard to create, I can help inspire people all over the world to be just a little bit healthier in their everyday lives.

Essential Tips for Getting Started

There are a few key things you should know before venturing out on your smoothie-bowl-making adventure. These essential tips detail the information necessary for making your bowls perfect every single time.

Prep Ahead: Prepare and gather all of your tools and ingredients before you begin. Wash and cut any fresh fruit, and grab your measuring cups and spatula so you're not searching for anything at the last minute.

Keep it Cool: Place your serving bowl in the freezer at least 30 minutes before blending to keep your frosty mixture from melting as soon as it hits the bowl. I like to store a bowl in the freezer at all times because you never know when a smoothie bowl craving will strike!

Bananarama: Ripe bananas work better in smoothie bowls because they're sweeter, so the more brown spots the better. To freeze, arrange peeled bananas (halved or quartered) on a parchment-lined sheet pan, then cover tightly with plastic wrap. When the bananas are frozen, transfer to a ziplock bag for longer storage.

Fat Equals Flavor: I recommend using unsweetened, full-fat canned coconut milk rather than the kind that comes in a carton, which is lighter and often contains sweeteners. Vigorously shake the can prior to opening to ensure it's well mixed. If it's still separated, pulse it in the blender for a few seconds to bring it back to a smooth consistency.

Apples to Apples: When making substitutions, always use similar ingredients. For example, swap nondairy milks with other nondairy milks, fruit juices with other fruit juices, berries with berries, etc.

Liquid Is the Enemy: The total amount of liquid needed will vary depending on several factors, such as which fruits and vegetables you're blending, how frozen they are, the other ingredients in the recipe, the type of blender you're using and the temperature of your kitchen. Start with less and add more a little at a time as needed.

Size Does Matter: Frozen fruit will blend easier if it starts out in small pieces rather than large chunks. Always cut ingredients into small pieces prior to freezing and/or blending.

Blender Basics: Use a high-powered blender or food processor for the best results. While a cheaper model can get the job done, a sturdy machine will make it a whole lot easier. The best model I've found for smoothie bowl making is the Vitamix Explorian Series E310 because it has a smaller blender jar plus a tamper tool. There are so many different high-quality blenders on the market today; do your own research and choose the model that's best for you.

Stop, Scrape, Repeat: Stop the blender often and use a rubber spatula to scrape down the sides. It may seem tedious, but doing this pushes ingredients toward the blade and helps to keep things moving. Otherwise, everything will just stick to the sides while the blades spin in the air. If your blender has a tamper tool or smoothie wand, use that to help move the ingredients around as they blend.

Be a Slacker: "Slack out" (partially defrost) your frozen ingredients for about 5 minutes before blending. Rock-solid frozen fruits, veggies and ice cubes will be much more difficult to blend and will often require more liquid.

Cubism: Freezing coffee, juices, nondairy milks and other liquids into ice cubes is an awesome way to add flavor and creaminess to your bowls without watering them down. Most standard ice cube trays produce 1-ounce (30-ml/2-tbsp) cubes, which is what I use and call for in this book. Adjust quantities as needed.

Keep it Short: Try not to blend for too long. As soon as the ingredients are fully blended and smooth, stop. Running the blender for too long will produce quite a bit of heat, which can cause the blended base to prematurely melt.

Blending Hack: If you have a food processor with a grater attachment, use it to shred your frozen fruit before blending. Grate the fruit right into the food processor, then swap out the grater attachment for the normal blade and blend it into a smooth, creamy mixture. The grater helps to quickly break down the fruit into smaller pieces so it blends faster and easier, often without the help of any liquid.

Fresh 'n Fruity

◂ ▲ ▸

Fruit is an essential part of any good smoothie bowl because it adds sweetness, acidity, flavor and texture. Also, fruits vary widely in their nutritional makeup, but nearly all of them are great sources of vitamins, minerals, antioxidants and fiber.

Just as in cooking, achieving a great-tasting smoothie bowl all comes down to balance. You want to match up the right flavors and textures to create a bowl that's not too sweet, sour, bitter, icy or watery. For example, a bowl made up of nothing but frozen blended raspberries would be overly acidic and full of pesky seeds, but if you add a banana, suddenly everything changes. The seedy texture is smoothed out and the acidity is mellowed by the banana's intense natural sweetness, making for a more balanced and much more pleasant-tasting bowl.

The recipes in this chapter are light, refreshing and fruit-forward, using everything from melons to citrus, berries to stone fruit and everything in between. You'll find some Soulberri classics, like our beloved Classic Açaí bowl (page 13) and the Party Wave (page 17), plus some of my personal favorites, like the Watermelon Creamsicle (page 14) and Blueberry Mango Lassi (page 18).

With the enormous variety of delicious, nutrient-dense fruits on the market, there are endless combinations of flavors, colors and textures just begging to be blended together. The bowls in this chapter are packed with vibrant, seasonal fruits in a rainbow of colors and flavors to please not only the eyes, tastebuds and tummy, but also the mind, body and soul.

Classic Açaí

Makes one bowl

FOR THE BASE
¼ cup (60 ml) apple juice, plus more as needed

1 (3.5-oz [100-g]) frozen packet unsweetened açaí purée

1 cup (150 g) frozen red seedless grapes

½ frozen banana

FOR TOPPING
¼ cup (35 g) Classic Granola (page 141)

½ banana, sliced

1 tbsp (15 ml) honey, or more or less to taste

This is the bowl that started it all! Açaí bowls went from an unknown item to a full-on phenomenon practically overnight. What started in Brazil spread to beach communities around the globe.

Frozen grapes are the secret ingredient in our Classic Açaí bowl at Soulberri. They provide natural sweetness and a juicy, refreshing texture that's somewhat similar to açaí, but a lot smoother. They pack a healthy dose of flavonoids and resveratrol to aid in both heart and brain health.

Add the apple juice to a blender or food processor. Break up the açaí packet into a few smaller pieces, then add it to the blender along with the frozen grapes and frozen banana. Blend on high, stopping to scrape down the sides with a rubber spatula every few minutes as needed. You may need to do this several times in order to get the mixture totally smooth. If you have a tamper tool, use it to help move the ingredients around as they blend. Add more apple juice in small amounts to help facilitate blending, but try to use as little liquid as possible in order to keep the mixture thick. Blend until it's as smooth as sorbet.

Transfer the mixture to a bowl, then sprinkle the granola over the top. Fan out the banana and arrange it along the side of the bowl, then drizzle all over with honey and serve immediately.

Ingredient Spotlight: Açaí. Pronounced ah-sigh-EEH, this deep purple berry comes from a palm tree native to South America. Açaí is considered a superfood due to its high concentration of antioxidants, fiber, calcium and omega-3 fatty acids. Packets of frozen açaí purée are the best resource for making açaí bowls.

Watermelon Creamsicle

Makes one bowl

FOR THE BASE

¼ cup (60 ml) orange juice, plus more as needed

2 (1-oz [30-ml]) coconut milk ice cubes (see tutorial on page 9)

2 cups (300 g) frozen watermelon chunks

FOR TOPPING

¼ cup (38 g) fresh watermelon chunks

½ tsp black sesame seeds

This bowl tastes like a cross between a snow cone and an orange creamsicle. I mashed two of my favorite childhood treats into one, only without any of the added sugar or artificial ingredients. This bowl has the most amazing slushy texture thanks to juicy frozen watermelon. It gets a hint of tang from orange juice, while coconut milk ice cubes add plenty of creaminess without watering it down.

I like to sprinkle this pretty pink bowl with black sesame seeds to mimic the black watermelon seeds that one rarely finds in a watermelon anymore. They also add a welcome crunchy bite. This bowl makes a wonderfully light afternoon snack, and it will leave you feeling hydrated and refreshed.

Add the orange juice, coconut milk ice cubes and frozen watermelon to a blender or food processor. Blend on high, using a tamper tool, if available, to smash down the ingredients and stopping to scrape down the sides as needed. Blend until the mixture is nice and smooth, like sorbet. If needed, add more orange juice, 1 tablespoon (15 ml) at a time, to help facilitate blending, but try to add as little as possible in order to keep the mixture thick.

Transfer the mixture to a bowl, then arrange the watermelon chunks on top. Sprinkle with black sesame seeds, then serve immediately.

Party Wave

Makes one bowl

FOR THE BASE
3 tbsp (45 ml) 100% unsweetened passion fruit juice or pulp (seeds removed if using fresh)

1 tbsp (15 ml) pineapple juice, plus more as needed

1 cup (150 g) frozen pineapple

1 cup (150 g) frozen mango

½ frozen banana

FOR TOPPING
¼ cup (35 g) Classic Granola (page 141)

½ banana, sliced

¼ cup (38 g) fresh pineapple chunks or slices

2 strawberries, hulled and sliced

½ kiwi, peeled and sliced

1 tbsp (9 g) unsweetened coconut flakes

This is one of our most popular bowls at Soulberri, right next to the Classic Açaí. Over the years it's developed an almost cult-like following.

This bowl has a custardy texture and tangy tropical flavor thanks to the addition of passion fruit, one of my all-time favorite ingredients. It is finished with a slew of fun, fruity toppings and tastes like a party wave in your mouth.

Add the passion fruit juice, pineapple juice, frozen pineapple, mango and banana to a blender or food processor. Blend on high, stopping to scrape down the sides every so often as needed. If a tamper tool is available, use it to help move the ingredients around as you blend. Add more pineapple juice, 1 tablespoon (15 ml) at a time as needed until the mixture is totally smooth, but try to add as little as possible to keep the mixture thick.

Transfer the mixture to a bowl, then sprinkle with the granola. Fan the banana out on top, then arrange the pineapple, strawberries and kiwi in rows or bunches. Sprinkle with coconut and serve immediately.

Tip: Always read the ingredients when purchasing passion fruit juice/pulp so you're getting 100% pure juice with no added sweeteners. Look for it in the freezer section and avoid the word "nectar," which typically indicates added sweeteners. Passion fruit juice/pulp is very sour and has a strong flavor, so unless you want to give your bowl a significant punch of tang, avoid adding more to your blend.

Blueberry Mango Lassi

Makes one bowl

FOR THE BASE

¼ cup (60 ml) apple juice, plus more as needed

½ cup (75 g) frozen blueberries

2 cups (300 g) frozen mango

¼ cup (63 g) plain Greek yogurt (see Tip)

⅛ tsp cardamom

1 tbsp (15 ml) honey

FOR TOPPING

¼ cup (35 g) Classic Granola (page 141)

¼ fresh mango, peeled and cut into chunks

¼ cup (38 g) fresh blueberries

2 tsp (10 ml) honey

This recipe draws its inspiration from mango lassi, a classic Indian drink made from mangoes and probiotic-rich yogurt. I add blueberries to give this bowl a gorgeous color, additional flavor and a boost in nutrition thanks to their high concentration of antioxidants. This bowl has a silky, creamy texture and tastes sweet and tangy with just a hint of spice.

A pinch of cardamom adds a warm and unusual flavor that sets this recipe apart from anything else. It's a very potent spice, so a little goes a long way.

Add the apple juice, frozen blueberries, frozen mango, yogurt, cardamom and honey to a blender or food processor. Blend on high, using a tamper tool, if available, to smash down the ingredients and help them move around. Stop and scrape down the sides as needed—you may need to do this several times. If the mixture is being stubborn, add 1 tablespoon (15 ml) of apple juice at a time to get things moving.

Transfer the mixture to a bowl, then sprinkle with the granola. Place the mangoes and blueberries over the top, drizzle with honey, then serve immediately.

Tip: I prefer plain, full-fat whole-milk yogurt, but feel free to use whichever kind you like. If using regular (non-Greek) yogurt, you may need to cut back a bit on the liquid as it contains more. For the best results, do not use vanilla, sweetened or flavored yogurt in this recipe. Nondairy yogurts may be substituted, but some work better than others, so experiment a little to find one that works best for you.

Lavender Cantaloupe

Makes one bowl

FOR THE BASE

¼ cup (60 ml) coconut milk, plus more as needed

1 tsp fresh lemon juice

2½ cups (375 g) frozen cantaloupe chunks

¼ tsp lavender flowers, or to taste

FOR TOPPING

¼ cup (38 g) fresh cantaloupe chunks or slices

1 tbsp (15 ml) honey

¼ tsp lavender flowers (optional)

Lavender is a lovely flavor that pairs well with many fruits. This recipe should be saved for the middle to end of summer when fresh melons are at their peak. I developed it using cantaloupe because it's widely available, but it would be wonderful with any of the unique and flavorful melon varieties that are available at farmers' markets throughout the season. A perfectly ripe summer melon should be sweet enough on its own, but if yours is lacking in flavor, feel free to sweeten it up with a little honey, agave nectar or maple syrup.

Add the coconut milk, lemon juice, frozen cantaloupe and lavender to a blender or food processor. Blend on high, using a tamper tool, if available, to smash down the ingredients and move them around. Stop to scrape down the sides as needed, and if the mixture is not blending well, add more coconut milk, 1 tablespoon (15 ml) at a time, just to get things going. Blend until the mixture is nice and smooth, like sorbet.

Transfer the mixture to a bowl, then arrange the cantaloupe chunks on top. Drizzle with honey, then sprinkle with lavender flowers. Serve immediately.

Tip: The potency of lavender flowers can vary widely. If your lavender is particularly fragrant, start with less, taste, then add more if desired.

Thai Mango Peanut

Makes one bowl

FOR THE BASE

¼ cup (60 ml) coconut milk, plus more as needed

1 tbsp (15 ml) fresh lime juice

1 tsp lime zest

2½ cups (375 g) frozen mango

2 tbsp (30 g) smooth peanut butter

2 tbsp (30 ml) honey

¼ tsp red pepper flakes, or more or less to taste

FOR TOPPING

1 tbsp (9 g) unsweetened coconut flakes or shavings

¼ mango, peeled and thinly sliced

Chili powder, for dusting (optional)

1 tbsp (9 g) salted, roasted peanuts, chopped

1 sprig Thai basil (optional)

This unique bowl was inspired by the flavors of Southeast Asia and one of my favorite condiments—spicy Thai peanut sauce. The base is made from mangoes and coconut milk, but it gets its kick of flavor from lime, peanut butter and chili flakes. It has a pleasant level of spice, which really adds an interesting feel to the bowl. If you're sensitive to spiciness, you can cut the amount of chili flakes in half, but I don't recommend omitting them completely. They give a very distinct flavor to this recipe that just isn't the same without them.

This bowl walks the line between sweet and savory and is so uniquely delicious. If you love a good spicy Thai peanut sauce, you will absolutely go crazy for this recipe.

Add the coconut milk, lime juice, lime zest, frozen mango, peanut butter, honey and red pepper flakes to a blender or food processor. Blend on high, using a tamper tool, if available, to smash down the ingredients and help move things around. Stop to scrape down the sides with a rubber spatula every so often as needed. Blend all of the ingredients until the mixture has the texture of ice cream.

Transfer the mixture to a bowl, smooth out the top, then sprinkle with the coconut flakes. Fan out the mango slices on top, then dust with a pinch of chili powder, if using. Sprinkle with chopped peanuts, then garnish with the Thai basil sprig, if desired. Serve immediately.

Southern Peach & Pecan

Makes one bowl

FOR THE BASE
2 tbsp (30 ml) apple juice, plus more as needed

2 cups (300 g) frozen sliced peaches (peeled)

½ cup (125 g) vanilla Greek yogurt

1 tbsp (15 ml) honey, or more or less, to taste

FOR TOPPING
¼ cup (38 g) Cinnamon Pecan Granola (page 145)

¼ fresh peach, sliced

1 tbsp (15 ml) honey

I was lucky enough to live in the beautiful state of Louisiana during my college years and was spoiled by the insanely flavorful southern peaches that come into season each summer. I've yet to experience a peach as good as the ones I tasted back then, but this bowl does a great job of capturing that incredible flavor and southern charm.

I recommend using store-bought frozen peaches for this recipe because they're widely available and so much easier than freezing them yourself. Because peaches have a fuzzy skin, you need to peel them prior to slicing and freezing, and I find that to be just a little too fussy. However, store-bought frozen peaches typically won't be the most flavorful, so if you have access to an abundance of sweet, peak-season southern peaches, it may be worth your while to freeze a batch so you can enjoy them long after the summer ends.

Add the apple juice, frozen peaches, yogurt and honey to a blender or food processor. Blend on high, using a tamper tool, if available, to smash the ingredients and help them blend. Stop and scrape down the sides every few minutes as needed. If the mixture isn't moving, you can add more apple juice, in 1 tablespoon (15 ml) increments, but try to use as little liquid as possible in order to keep it nice and thick. Blend until the mixture is nice and smooth, like sorbet.

Transfer the mixture to a bowl, then sprinkle the Cinnamon Pecan Granola over the top. Fan out the peach slices and arrange them on the bowl, then drizzle with honey. Serve immediately.

Cotton Candy Grape

Makes one bowl

FOR THE BASE

¼ cup (60 ml) coconut milk, plus more as needed

2 cups (300 g) frozen cotton candy grapes

½ (1.7-oz [50-g]) frozen packet unsweetened pitaya (dragon fruit) purée

½ frozen banana

¼ tsp vanilla extract

FOR TOPPING

1 strawberry, hulled and sliced

3 white pitaya (dragon fruit) hearts

1 tsp unsweetened coconut flakes

Cotton candy grapes were created using cross-pollination techniques, so their flavor is surprisingly all natural and not due to any artificial flavoring. Because these fruits are considered somewhat of a specialty, you'll need to seek them out and freeze them yourself prior to making this recipe. It's worth it! This frosty, refreshing bowl will make you feel like a kid in a candy store. If you can't find cotton candy grapes, feel free to substitute standard green grapes.

Add the coconut milk, frozen cotton candy grapes, frozen pitaya purée, frozen banana and vanilla to a blender or food processor. Blend on high, using a tamper tool, if available, to smash down the ingredients, stopping to scrape down the sides as needed. Blend until the mixture is nice and smooth.

Transfer the mixture to a bowl, smooth out the top, then arrange the strawberry slices and pitaya hearts in a circle on top. Sprinkle with the coconut flakes, then serve immediately.

Tip: Frozen pitaya (dragon fruit) packets may be purchased at health-food stores, upscale food markets and online. Be sure to look for 100% pure, unsweetened pitaya.

Pro Styling Tip: Slice the fresh pitaya about ½ inch (13 mm) thick, then use a small heart-shaped cookie cutter to create the pitaya hearts. Alternatively, you can use a sharp paring knife to hand-cut the shapes.

Blueberry Pancakes

Makes one bowl

FOR THE BASE

¼ cup (60 ml) almond milk, plus more as needed

1 frozen banana

1 cup (150 g) frozen blueberries

2 (1-oz [30-ml]) almond milk ice cubes (see tutorial on page 9)

1 tbsp (9 g) chopped pecans

1 tbsp (15 ml) maple syrup

¼ tsp cinnamon

FOR TOPPING

¼ cup (38 g) Cinnamon Pecan Granola (page 145)

¼ cup (38 g) fresh blueberries

2 tsp (10 ml) maple syrup

Pansies or other edible flowers, for garnish (optional)

Practically all smoothie bowls are great for breakfast, but this one really takes the cake . . . I mean pancake. The base is made with bananas, blueberries, almond milk ice cubes and pecans to produce a substantial consistency, a bright blueberry flavor and beautiful periwinkle color. A splash of maple syrup and a pinch of cinnamon really drive home that unmistakable breakfast taste.

The floral garnish is by no means necessary, but if you have some (pesticide-free) edible flowers, like pansies or nasturtiums, growing in your garden, they make this bowl even more fun to eat.

Add the almond milk, frozen banana, frozen blueberries, almond milk ice cubes, pecans, maple syrup and cinnamon to a blender or food processor. Blend on high, scraping down the sides as needed and using a tamper tool, if available, to smash down the ingredients and facilitate blending. Add more almond milk, 1 tablespoon (15 ml) at a time as needed to help get things moving.

Transfer the mixture to a bowl, sprinkle with the Cinnamon Pecan Granola and place the blueberries on top. Drizzle with the maple syrup, garnish with an edible flower (optional), then serve immediately.

Pom-Berry Yogurt

Makes one bowl

FOR THE BASE
¼ cup (60 ml) pomegranate juice, plus more as needed

¾ cup (115 g) frozen blueberries

¾ cup (115 g) frozen strawberries

1 frozen banana

¼ cup (63 g) vanilla Greek yogurt

FOR TOPPING
¼ cup (38 g) Classic Granola (page 141)

1 fresh strawberry, hulled and sliced

¼ cup (38 g) fresh or frozen blueberries

2 tbsp (20 g) pomegranate seeds

This smooth and tangy treat is packed with both flavor and health, thanks to the loads of natural antioxidants and fiber found in the berries and pomegranate. Both blueberries and pomegranates are considered "superfoods" because they cram so many nutrients into tiny packages. Greek yogurt provides a generous amount of protein, so it will help keep you fuller longer, in addition to having plenty of gut-aiding probiotics. This is one of my favorite bowls to enjoy for breakfast because it's not too sweet and contains so much good stuff.

Add the pomegranate juice, frozen blueberries, frozen strawberries, frozen banana and Greek yogurt to a blender or food processor. Blend on high, scraping down the sides as needed until the mixture is smooth and creamy. You will need to stop and scrape several times in order to get the mixture totally smooth. Add more pomegranate juice 1 tablespoon (15 ml) at a time just to get it moving, but try to use as little liquid as possible in order to keep it nice and thick. If you have a tamper tool available, use it to help facilitate blending.

Transfer the mixture to a bowl, then sprinkle with the granola. Arrange the strawberries, blueberries and pomegranate seeds on top, then serve immediately.

Pro Styling Tip: In order to achieve a chilly, whimsical look, top your bowls with frozen fruit instead of fresh. Frozen fruits give a more pastel, frosted look to the bowl that can be very attractive in certain instances. Frozen fruits will have a different texture though, so it all comes down to personal preference.

Passionate Papaya

Makes one bowl

FOR THE BASE
2 tbsp (30 ml) pineapple juice, plus more as needed

2 tbsp (30 ml) 100% unsweetened passion fruit juice or pulp (seeds removed if using fresh)

1½ cups (225 g) frozen papaya chunks

1 frozen banana

FOR TOPPING
½ banana, sliced

¼ cup (38 g) fresh papaya chunks

1 tbsp (15 ml) fresh passion fruit pulp (with or without seeds) (optional)

Passion fruit is one of my all time favorite fruit flavors, but it can be challenging (and expensive!) to find fresh. I always keep blocks of 100% pure passion fruit pulp in my freezer as an easy way to add vibrant flavor to all sorts of recipes, especially smoothie bowls.

Papaya makes a wonderful base for a bowl because, when frozen and blended, it has a creamy texture and a fairly mild flavor that pairs especially well with other tropical fruits.

Add the pineapple juice, passion fruit juice, frozen papaya and frozen banana to a blender or food processor. Blend on high, stopping to scrape down the sides every few seconds as needed. If your blender has a tamper tool, use it to smash down the ingredients and move them around. Add more pineapple juice, 1 tablespoon (15 ml) at a time, to help the mixture blend, but use as little liquid as possible in order to keep the mixture nice and thick. Blend until totally smooth.

Transfer the mixture to a bowl, then fan out the banana over the top and place the papaya chunks right next to the banana. Drizzle passion fruit pulp in the center, if desired, then serve immediately.

Tip: Always read ingredients when purchasing passion fruit juice/pulp so you're only getting 100% pure juice with no added sweeteners. Look for it in the freezer section and avoid the word "nectar," which typically indicates added sweeteners. Passion fruit juice/pulp is very sour and has a strong flavor, so unless you want to give your bowl a significant punch of tang, avoid adding any more than called for to your blend.

Strawberry Orange Banana Swirl

Makes one bowl

FOR THE BASE
4 tbsp (60 ml) orange juice, divided

1½ frozen bananas

1 cup (150 g) frozen strawberries

FOR TOPPING
¼ cup (38 g) Classic Granola (page 141)

½ banana, sliced

2-3 fresh strawberries, hulled and sliced

This is what I would consider an "evergreen" smoothie bowl. The ingredients are easy to find and the flavors are welcome pretty much any time of year. Swirling the colors is an optional way to make this basic bowl a little more fun and interesting, but it doesn't change the flavor at all. If you'd rather keep it easy, just throw everything in the blender at the same time and have at it.

Add 2 tablespoons (30 ml) of orange juice and the frozen bananas to a blender or food processor. Blend on high, using a tamper tool, if available, to smash down the ingredients to help them blend and stopping to scrape down the sides as needed. Once smooth, transfer three quarters of the mixture to one side of a serving bowl, then place the bowl in the freezer.

Add the strawberries and remaining 2 tablespoons (30 ml) of orange juice to the blender with the remaining banana mixture and continue blending until totally smooth. Remove the bowl from the freezer and add the strawberry mixture to the other side. You may need to move some of the banana mixture over in order to make room.

Use the back of a spoon to quickly, but artfully, blend the two colors together, creating a fun swirly pattern. Sprinkle granola over one side only so you can see the fun pattern, then place the banana and strawberry slices on top of the granola. Serve immediately.

Sunshine Citrus

Makes one bowl

FOR THE BASE
½ small fresh grapefruit or ¼ large grapefruit, peeled, seeds and pith removed

1 medium orange, peeled, seeds and pith removed

1 cup (150 g) frozen pineapple

½ frozen banana

Orange, grapefruit or pineapple juice, only if needed

FOR TOPPING
4 orange segments

4 grapefruit segments

½ tsp bee pollen (see Ingredient Spotlight on page 62)

Dried Pineapple Flower (page 167) (optional)

If you want to eat a bowl that tastes like a bright sunny day, look no further. One of the few silver linings to a cold, bleak winter is that citrus is in peak season. When there's snow on the ground and your body is craving sunlight and vitamin C, this bowl is just the thing to awaken all your senses and nourish your soul.

This recipe doesn't call for the addition of any liquid because the fresh orange and grapefruit provide plenty. However, if your blender is having trouble breaking everything down, feel free to add a splash of orange juice, grapefruit juice or pineapple juice to get things moving. This light and refreshing bowl keeps the toppings simple with some additional citrus segments and a little sprinkle of immune-boosting bee pollen. The pineapple flower makes a gorgeous garnish, but is by no means necessary.

Add the grapefruit, orange, frozen pineapple and frozen banana to a blender or food processor. Blend on high, using a tamper tool, if available, to smash down the ingredients and stopping to scrape down the sides every so often as needed. Blend until smooth, like sorbet. If the ingredients aren't blending, add a splash of orange, grapefruit or pineapple juice just to get things moving.

Transfer the mixture to a bowl, smooth out the top, then arrange the orange and grapefruit segments in an alternating pattern. Sprinkle with bee pollen, garnish with a pineapple flower, if desired, and serve immediately.

Blueberry Barrel

Makes one bowl

FOR THE BASE
¼ cup (60 ml) apple juice, plus more as needed

½ frozen banana

2 cups (300 g) frozen blueberries

FOR TOPPING
¼ cup (38 g) Classic Granola (page 141)

¼ cup (38 g) fresh blueberries

1 tbsp (9 g) sliced or slivered almonds

After our first season at Soulberri, I wanted to expand our menu, but still wanted to keep it fairly small since we operate out of such a tight space. To compensate, I removed one of our lower-selling bowls to make room for the new ones. When we released the new menu, there was a massive uproar from the community and I immediately knew I'd made a mistake. We brought it back as a secret menu item and it's had a strong following ever since.

The idea behind this bowl was to take the concept of the ever-popular açaí bowl, but tweak it to use locally sourced ingredients instead. Southern New Jersey is known for producing some of the best (and most) blueberries in the world, and because blueberries are known for being an incredibly good source of antioxidants, I saw them as a perfect replacement for açaí.

Add the apple juice, frozen banana and frozen blueberries to a blender or food processor. Blend on high, scraping down the sides as needed and using a tamper tool, if available, to smash down the ingredients and facilitate blending. Add more apple juice, 1 tablespoon (15 ml) at a time, to help get things moving, but try to use as little liquid as possible to keep the mixture thick.

Transfer the mixture to a bowl, sprinkle with the granola, then add the blueberries on top. Sprinkle with the almonds and serve immediately.

Pitaya en la Playa

Makes one bowl

The pitaya (aka dragon fruit) bowl has quickly been gaining traction thanks to its smooth texture, pleasantly sweet flavor and knock-out gorgeous fluorescent pink color. This bowl has a sweet tropical flavor, is topped with a rainbow of beautiful fresh fruits and will make you feel like you're on a beach that's covered with flamingos.

FOR THE BASE

¼ cup (60 ml) apple juice, plus more as needed

1 (3.5-oz [100-g]) frozen packet unsweetened pitaya (dragon fruit) purée

1 frozen banana

½ cup (75 g) frozen pineapple

½ cup (75 g) frozen mango

FOR TOPPING

¼ cup (38 g) sliced pineapple

¼ cup (38 g) cubed mango

½ kiwi, peeled and sliced

1 tsp unsweetened coconut flakes

Add the apple juice to a blender or food processor. Break up the pitaya packet into a few smaller pieces, then add it to the blender along with the frozen banana, frozen pineapple and frozen mango. Blend on high, stopping to scrape down the sides every few seconds, using a tamper tool, if available, to help move things around. Add more apple juice, 1 tablespoon (15 ml) at a time, as needed to help facilitate blending, but try to add as little liquid as possible. Blend until the mixture is totally smooth and resembles a thick sorbet.

Transfer the mixture to a bowl, then arrange the pineapple, mango and kiwi on top in rows. Sprinkle with coconut flakes, then serve immediately.

Ingredient Spotlight: Pitaya. This crazy-looking cactus fruit, also known as "dragon fruit," has a vibrant pink exterior with green leaf-like extensions, but the inside can vary. Some are bright white and speckled with tiny black seeds, while others are a deep magenta. Most pitaya bowls use a frozen purée—similar to açaí—which is always made from the pink variety, giving the bowls that distinct neon hue. Look for frozen pitaya packets at health-food stores, upscale food markets and online, and always make sure you're buying 100% pure, unsweetened pitaya. Find fresh white or pink fleshed dragon fruit at specialty produce shops, Asian markets and online.

Super Bowls

◀ ▲ ▶

The phrase "Super Bowl" doesn't just refer to the biggest sporting event in America, it also represents a smoothie bowl that has just a little more to offer. Whether they're loaded with supplements to make you look and feel your best, or with a shot of caffeine to help get your day started, each bowl in this chapter has something in it that makes it "super."

One of the things I love most about smoothie bowls is that you can sneak in so many add-ins and extras to up the health factor without really affecting the overall flavor. Smoothie bowls are such a delicious way to cram as many fruits, veggies and nutrients into your diet as possible without really feeling like you're doing so. Instead of choking down a salad for breakfast, I'd way rather eat a yummy frozen treat.

I love starting my day with a caffeinated bowl, whether it's with coffee, chai tea or matcha. The caffeine gives me the jolt I need to start my day, while the protein and fiber ensure I'll stay full until at least lunchtime.

You may think that some of the bowls like Unicorn Kisses (page 57) and Starry Night (page 45) are considered "super" mostly for their looks, but don't judge these books by their covers. We all know it's what's inside that counts, and these bowls are all loaded with healthy add-ins like spirulina, activated charcoal, bee pollen and hemp seed to give their nutritional profiles a major boost.

You can really have fun with some of these colorful ingredients to create a masterpiece worthy of being in a museum—or at the very least, your Instagram feed.

Starry Night

Makes one bowl

Just like the famous Van Gogh painting, this Starry Night smoothie bowl is easily one of the prettiest bowls you can make, and it also happens to be one of my favorites to eat. I use two different colors to make the unique swirly pattern, which is what gives it that awesome outer space feel. Blue spirulina helps make the pretty blue color, while blueberries bring in the dark, deep purple. Coconut flakes and bee pollen look like tiny stars in the sky, but it's the star-shaped pieces of fruit that really make the picture come alive.

FOR THE BASE

4 tbsp (60 ml) apple juice, divided, plus more as needed

1½ frozen bananas

½ tsp blue spirulina (see Ingredient Spotlight on page 57)

1 cup (150 g) frozen blueberries

FOR TOPPING

1 tsp unsweetened coconut flakes

½ tsp bee pollen (see Ingredient Spotlight on page 62)

2 slices star fruit

3 white pitaya (dragon fruit) stars (see Pro Styling Tip on page 26)

Add 2 tablespoons (30 ml) of the apple juice, frozen bananas and blue spirulina to a blender or food processor. Blend on high, using a tamper tool (if available) to help smash down the bananas and mix everything around. Stop and scrape down the sides as needed, then, once fully blended, transfer three quarters of the mixture to a cup or bowl (not the serving bowl) and place it in the freezer.

Add the frozen blueberries and the remaining 2 tablespoons (30 ml) of apple juice to the remaining banana mixture, then blend on high, adding more apple juice, 1 tablespoon (15 ml) at a time, as needed, until totally smooth.

Transfer the blueberry mixture to a serving bowl and smooth it out into an even layer. Take the banana/spirulina mixture out of the freezer and dot it in two or three different spots on top of the blueberry mixture, then use the back of a small spoon to quickly, but gently, mix the colors around and create a swirly, spacelike design.

Sprinkle with coconut flakes and bee pollen, then arrange the star fruit and pitaya stars on top. Serve immediately.

Berries 'n 'Booch

Makes one bowl

FOR THE BASE
¼ cup (60 ml) kombucha, plus more as needed

4 (1-oz [30-ml]) kombucha ice cubes (see Tip)

½ frozen banana

¾ cup (115 g) frozen strawberries

¾ cup (115 g) frozen blueberries

FOR TOPPING
2 strawberries, sliced

5 raspberries

5 blueberries

Tip: Frozen kombucha ice cubes allow for more of that kombucha flavor without watering down the bowl. Gently stir the kombucha, then freeze it in ice cube trays until solid. Transfer the frozen cubes to a ziplock bag and keep them on hand for future smoothie bowls or for icing down a cold glass of 'booch!

'Booch is an affectionate nickname for kombucha, the fizzy fermented beverage that's become super popular in recent years. It's made from tea and has a sour flavor that pairs really well with fruit. Kombucha, like other fermented foods, is loaded with gut-healthy probiotics as well as prebiotics, aka the food necessary for probiotics to thrive in the body. Many people brew their own kombucha at home, but it's widely available at health-food stores, and many traditional grocery stores now carry it as well.

Most of kombucha's natural effervescence is lost in the blending process, but it still has that signature tang that makes your taste buds sing. I used an unflavored kombucha to create this recipe to keep the flavor neutral, but it would work nicely with any of the different flavored varieties available on the market. Ginger and berry flavors would be especially nice.

Add the kombucha, kombucha ice cubes, frozen banana, frozen strawberries and frozen blueberries to a blender or food processor. Blend on high, using a tamper tool, if available, to smash down the ingredients and stopping to scrape down the sides as needed. Blend until the mixture is nice and smooth, adding more kombucha, 1 tablespoon (15 ml) at a time, just to get everything moving.

Transfer the mixture to a bowl, smooth it out, then arrange the strawberries, raspberries and blueberries in stripes on top. Serve immediately.

Maca Mocha Loca

Makes one bowl

FOR THE BASE

¼ cup (60 ml) coconut milk, plus more as needed

¼ tsp vanilla extract

2 frozen bananas

4 (1-oz [30-ml]) coffee ice cubes (see tutorial on page 9)

1 large date, soaked in hot water for 10 minutes, then drained

1 tsp maca powder

1 tbsp (8 g) cacao powder or good-quality cocoa powder (see Ingredient Spotlight on page 154)

FOR TOPPING

2 tbsp (30 ml) Chocolate Magic (page 162), divided

¼ cup (38 g) Chocolate Almond Granola (page 142)

Try saying that name three times fast! The base of this incredibly healthy bowl tastes like chocolate ice cream, but it's the toppings that really set it apart. A scoop of Chocolate Almond Granola (page 142) adds a delicious crunch, while a drizzle of Chocolate Magic (page 162) adds melt-in-your mouth texture, in addition to healthy fats, which make all those nutrients even more bioavailable.

Add the coconut milk, vanilla extract, frozen bananas, coffee ice cubes, date, maca powder and cacao powder to a blender or food processor. Blend on high, using a tamper tool, if available, to smash down the ingredients and stopping to scrape down the sides as needed. Blend all of the ingredients until the mixture is nice and smooth, adding more coconut milk, 1 tablespoon (15 ml) at a time, as needed to get everything moving.

Transfer half of the mixture to a bowl, then drizzle 1 tablespoon (15 ml) of Chocolate Magic on top. Place the rest of the mixture on top, smooth it out, then drizzle with the remaining 1 tablespoon (15 ml) of Chocolate Magic and place in the freezer for 30 seconds to set. Sprinkle with the Chocolate Almond Granola, then serve immediately.

Ingredient Spotlight: Maca. This ancient superfood is a South American root that looks like a turnip and has a mild ginger flavor. High in essential fatty acids, vitamins, minerals and antioxidants, it's said to increase energy, immune function and mental clarity. Maca is sold as a powder or in pill form and is best blended into a smoothie bowl base.

Blue Suede

Makes one bowl

FOR THE BACON TOPPING (OPTIONAL)
1 slice responsibly sourced bacon

FOR THE BASE
¼ cup (60 ml) coconut milk, plus more as needed

2½ frozen bananas

¼ tsp vanilla extract

¼ tsp blue spirulina (see Ingredient Spotlight on page 57)

FOR TOPPING
1 tbsp (15 g) Peanut Butter Magic (page 162)

¼ cup (35 g) Classic Granola (page 141)

½ banana, sliced

1 tbsp (15 g) peanut butter, smooth or crunchy

2 tsp (10 ml) honey

This is my ode to the King. I've always shared in Elvis's love of the fried peanut butter, bacon and banana sandwich, so this is essentially that—only in smoothie bowl form. A little bit of crumbled, crispy bacon sprinkled on top is what gives this bowl the most incredible explosion of salty-sweet flavor. If you don't eat meat, the bacon can be easily replaced with a plant-based bacon alternative or omitted completely. Some salty roasted peanuts would also make an excellent vegan swap.

Preheat an oven or toaster oven to 350°F (180°C). Place the bacon slice on a small sheet pan, then bake until crisp, about 20 minutes. Drain on paper towels, let cool, then chop or crumble and set aside.

Add the coconut milk, frozen bananas, vanilla and blue spirulina to a blender or food processor. Blend on high, scraping down the sides as needed until nice and smooth. If you have a tamper tool available, use it to move around the ingredients and mash them down. If the mixture is not blending well, add more coconut milk, 1 tablespoon (15 ml) at a time, to help things along.

Transfer half of the mixture to a bowl, drizzle with the Peanut Butter Magic, then top with the remaining smoothie mixture. Sprinkle with the Classic Granola, then arrange the banana slices on top. Slather with the peanut butter, sprinkle with bacon bits, drizzle with honey, then serve immediately.

Tip: A little bit of blue spiruluna is used to color the base to give it a lovely pale blue hue, hence the name of this recipe. You can leave it out with no change to the flavor, but I just couldn't resist!

Morning Glory

Makes one bowl

FOR THE BASE

¼ cup (60 ml) apple juice, plus more as needed

2 (1-oz [30-ml]) coconut milk ice cubes (see tutorial on page 9)

½ cup (75 g) frozen apple chunks, peeled

½ cup (75 g) frozen pineapple

½ cup (75 g) frozen chopped carrots

½ cup (68 g) frozen banana

2 tbsp (18 g) walnuts

1 date, soaked in boiling water for 10 minutes, then drained

½ tsp vanilla extract

½ tsp cinnamon

1 tsp maca powder (see Ingredient Spotlight on page 49)

Pinch of salt

FOR TOPPING

¼ apple, cored and thinly sliced

Cinnamon, for dusting

2 tbsp (20 g) Bird Seed Brittle (page 150), crumbled

1 tbsp (9 g) sunflower seeds

Inspired by morning glory muffins, this bowl is packed with similar ingredients for a frozen version of this classic coffee house breakfast treat. It has apples, carrots, pineapple, banana, walnuts, dates and a spoonful of maca, a South American superfood that adds an energizing element and slight ginger flavor.

Frozen chopped carrots are an incredible resource to keep on hand for smoothies and bowls like this one. They're already peeled, chopped and blanched, so they are easier to break down in a blend, and since carrots are naturally sweet, they blend beautifully into many different recipes.

This bowl has such a varied mix of different flavors and textures and is loaded with fiber and nutrients that will help you power through your day.

Add the apple juice, coconut milk ice cubes, frozen apple, frozen pineapple, frozen carrots, frozen banana, walnuts, date, vanilla, cinnamon, maca and salt to a blender or food processor. Blend on high, using a tamper tool, if available, to smash down the ingredients and stopping to scrape down the sides as needed. Blend all of the ingredients until the mixture is nice and smooth, adding more apple juice, 1 tablespoon (15 ml) at a time, as needed to help things move around.

Transfer the mixture to a bowl, then smooth out the top. Arrange the apple slices on top, then dust with the cinnamon. Sprinkle with the Bird Seed Brittle and sunflower seeds, then serve immediately.

Magical Mermaid

Makes one bowl

FOR THE BASE
¼ cup (60 ml) coconut milk, plus more as needed

1½ frozen bananas

1 cup (150 g) frozen pineapple

1 large handful kale (2–3 leaves with tender stems), torn into pieces

FOR TOPPING
1 tbsp (15 g) Coconut Magic (page 162)

¼ tsp blue-green spirulina (optional)

¼ cup (38 g) fresh or frozen blueberries

1 tbsp (9 g) unsweetened coconut flakes

1 tsp Power Seed Sprinkle (page 149)

This bowl will have you feeling like a beautiful mermaid inside and out. It's both powered by, and decorated with, blue-green spirulina. This bowl also has a little bit of Coconut Magic (page 162), which is such a fun textural experience that once you try it, it's hard to enjoy a bowl without it.

Add the coconut milk, frozen bananas, frozen pineapple and kale to a blender or food processor. Blend on high, using a tamper tool, if available, to smash down the ingredients and stopping to scrape down the sides as needed. Blend until the mixture is nice and smooth, adding more coconut milk, 1 tablespoon (15 ml) at a time, just to get everything moving.

Transfer half of the smoothie mixture to a serving bowl, then drizzle with the Coconut Magic, then spoon all but 2 tablespoons (30 g) of the remaining mixture on top. Transfer the bowl to the freezer.

Use a spoon to mix together the last 2 tablespoons (30 g) of the mixture with the spirulina in a small bowl until totally combined. It should be a deep green color.

Remove the bowl from the freezer, then drizzle the top with the spirulina mixture. Use the back of a spoon to carefully, but quickly, create a swirled pattern. Sprinkle with blueberries, coconut flakes and Power Seed Sprinkle, then serve immediately.

Ingredient Spotlight: Blue-Green Spirulina.

This powerful superfood is a natural algae powder that's one of the most nutrient-dense foods on the planet. It's incredibly high in protein and a good source of antioxidants, iron, calcium and other vitamins, minerals and phytonutrients.

Unicorn Kisses

Makes one bowl

This bowl is not only one of the most beautiful to make, it's also packed with a ton of stealthy nutrition. This recipe was created as a variation on the Unicorn Smoothie, which is a popular choice for kids at Soulberri. It uses all-natural ingredients rather than food coloring to create the pretty pastel design.

FOR THE BASE

¼ cup (60 ml) apple juice, plus more as needed

1½ frozen bananas

1 cup (150 g) frozen strawberries

⅛ tsp blue spirulina

FOR TOPPING

½ tsp bee pollen (see Ingredient Spotlight on page 62)

1 tbsp (3 g) puffed millet (see Ingredient Spotlight on page 125)

½ banana, sliced

1 strawberry, sliced in half

2 tbsp (30 ml) Coconut Whipped Cream (page 157)

Pitaya powder, for dusting (optional) (see Tip)

Chamomile flowers or other edible flowers, for garnish (optional)

Add the apple juice, frozen bananas and frozen strawberries to a blender or food processor. Blend on high, using a tamper tool, if available, to smash down the ingredients and stopping to scrape down the sides as needed. Blend until the mixture is nice and smooth, adding more apple juice, 1 tablespoon (15 ml) at a time, as needed.

Transfer three quarters of the smoothie mixture to a bowl, then place it in the freezer. Add the blue spirulina to the remainder of the smoothie mixture in the blender or processor, and blend until fully incorporated—the mixture should turn purple. Remove the bowl from the freezer, then add a few dollops of the purple mixture to the top. Use a spoon to lift the pink parts to blend with the blue and create a swirly pattern.

Sprinkle with the bee pollen and puffed millet, then arrange the banana and strawberry slices on top. Place a dollop of Coconut Whipped Cream on one side of the bowl, dust with pitaya powder, garnish with chamomile flowers, then serve immediately.

Tip: If pitaya powder is unavailable, you can substitute hibiscus powder. You can also omit this ingredient and still have good results.

Ingredient Spotlight: Blue Spirulina. Just like its blue-green counterpart, blue spirulina is derived from algae, only this version produces a clean blue color. Don't substitute blue-green spirulina or it will turn the mixture brown rather than purple.

Black Magic

Makes one bowl

FOR THE BASE

¼ cup (60 ml) Concord grape juice, plus more as needed

1½ cups (225 g) frozen blueberries

½ cup (75 g) frozen cherries

½ cup (75 g) frozen blackberries

½ tsp activated charcoal powder

½ tsp blue-green spirulina (see Ingredient Spotlight on page 54)

FOR TOPPING

5 fresh blackberries

Smoothie bowls are easily one of the most photogenic foods on the planet, which is one of the reasons why I think they're so popular. They're always full of such brilliant colors, so I took on the challenge of making a bowl that's totally black. Frozen blueberries, cherries, blackberries and activated charcoal give this bowl its deep, dark hue, while the blue-green spirulina neutralizes the purple tones. In sticking with the theme, it is garnished simply, with just a handful of blackberries, but you can embellish it with whichever toppings your heart desires.

Add the Concord grape juice, frozen blueberries, frozen cherries, frozen blackberries, charcoal powder and spirulina to a blender or food processor. Blend on high, using a tamper tool, if available, to smash down the ingredients and stopping to scrape down the sides as needed. Blend until the mixture is nice and smooth, like sorbet, adding more grape juice, 1 tablespoon (15 ml) at a time, to help get things moving.

Transfer the mixture to a bowl, smooth out the top, then dot with the blackberries. Serve immediately.

Ingredient Spotlight: Activated Charcoal.

This is a fun ingredient that boasts many different benefits, from whitening teeth to detoxifying the body. Here it's used purely for aesthetics. Activated charcoal can interact with some medications, so check with a healthcare professional before consuming if you're not sure.

Cool Buzz

Makes one bowl

FOR THE BASE

¼ cup (60 ml) coconut milk, plus more as needed

¼ tsp vanilla extract

1 tbsp (15 ml) maple syrup

2 frozen bananas

4 (1-oz [30-ml]) coffee ice cubes (see tutorial on page 9)

¼ cup (35 g) raw cashews, soaked overnight and drained

FOR TOPPING

2 tbsp (30 ml) Vanilla Cashew Butter Drizzle (page 165)

¼ cup (38 g) Super Seed Granola (page 146)

½ banana, sliced

We have a smoothie at Soulberri called the Cool Buzz, named after the infamous line from Sean Penn's character Jeff Spicoli in the classic '80s movie, *Fast Times at Ridgemont High*. "All I need are some tasty waves, a cool buzz and I'm fine." The Soulberri version is made with cold-brewed coffee, cashews, banana and vanilla. This is a thicker version, only with toppings galore—aka, those tasty waves!

Add the coconut milk, vanilla, maple syrup, frozen bananas, coffee ice cubes and drained soaked cashews to a blender or food processor. Blend on high, using a tamper tool, if available, to smash down the ingredients and stopping to scrape down the sides as needed. Blend until the mixture is nice and smooth, like ice cream, adding more coconut milk, 1 tablespoon (15 ml) at a time, just to get everything moving.

Transfer the mixture to a bowl, smooth out the top, then drizzle with Vanilla Cashew Butter Drizzle. Top with Super Seed Granola, then fan out the banana slices and serve immediately.

Tip: Pour leftover strongly brewed coffee into ice-cube trays. When frozen, store them in a ziplock bag for making smoothie bowls.

Busy Bee

Makes one bowl

This bowl has a secret kick of caffeine from coffee, but the flavor is mellowed by the almond butter and honey. I've added a double dose of bee pollen into this recipe, which is the real superstar ingredient here.

FOR THE BASE
¼ cup (60 ml) almond milk, plus more as needed

1 frozen banana

4 (1-oz [30-ml]) coffee ice cubes (see tutorial on page 9)

2 (1-oz [30-ml]) almond milk ice cubes (see tutorial on page 9)

1 tbsp (15 ml) raw honey

2 tbsp (30 g) almond butter

1 tsp bee pollen

FOR TOPPING
¼ cup (38 g) Classic Granola (page 141)

½ banana, sliced

1 tbsp (15 g) almond butter

1 tbsp (15 ml) honey

½ tsp bee pollen

Add the almond milk, frozen banana, coffee ice cubes, almond milk ice cubes, honey, almond butter and bee pollen to a blender or food processor. Blend on high, using a tamper tool, if available, to smash down the ingredients and stopping to scrape down the sides as needed. Blend all of the ingredients until the mixture is nice and smooth, adding more almond milk, 1 tablespoon (15 ml) at a time, to help facilitate blending.

Transfer the mixture to a bowl, smooth out the top, then sprinkle with granola. Fan the banana slices on top, then drizzle with almond butter and honey. Sprinkle with bee pollen and serve immediately.

Ingredient Spotlight: Bee Pollen. This superfood
is actually the pollen collected from bees that's been packed and concentrated in the hive for use by the queen bee. It contains protein, B vitamins, essential minerals and, if sourced locally, has been said to help combat seasonal allergies. It has a beautiful mustardy color that looks pretty sprinkled on top of bowls and has a uniquely floral flavor and powdery texture. Look for it at health-food stores and farmers' markets.

Banana Chai Oatmeal

Makes one bowl

FOR THE BASE
¼ cup (60 ml) almond milk, plus more as needed

2 tbsp (18 g) rolled oats (see Tips)

1½ frozen bananas

3 (1-oz [30-ml]) strongly brewed chai tea ice cubes (see Tips)

2 (1-oz [30-ml]) almond milk ice cubes (see tutorial on page 9)

1 tbsp (15 ml) honey

¼ tsp vanilla extract

FOR TOPPING
2 tbsp (30 ml) Cinnamon Almond Butter Drizzle (page 166)

½ banana, sliced

1 tbsp (9 g) Sweet Dukkah (page 153)

Everything about this bowl says warm and toasty, except for the fact that it's frozen.

Strongly brewed chai tea ice cubes give this bowl a beautifully spiced base along with a kick of caffeine, making it a great choice for breakfast. What really brings it over the edge is the toppings, which gives it a boost of flavor and a unique nutty crunch.

Add the almond milk, oats, frozen bananas, chai tea ice cubes, almond milk ice cubes, honey and vanilla to a blender or food processor. Let sit for 5 minutes so the oats can absorb some of the almond milk and the ice cubes can slack out a bit. Blend on high, using a tamper tool, if available, to smash down the ingredients and stopping to scrape down the sides as needed. Blend until the mixture is nice and smooth, adding more almond milk, 1 tablespoon (15 ml) at a time, just to get everything moving.

Transfer the mixture to a bowl, then swirl in the Cinnamon Almond Butter Drizzle. Arrange the banana slices on top, sprinkle with the Sweet Dukkah, then serve immediately.

Tips: Use certified gluten-free oats if you are keeping totally gluten free (see Ingredient Spotlight on page 141).

For this recipe, it's important to brew a batch of chai tea that's so strong it's unpleasant to drink on its own. I use four parts water to one part tea and let it steep for 30 minutes, then freeze into ice cubes so that it doesn't water down the recipe.

Super Green Protein

FOR THE BASE

¼ cup (60 ml) almond milk, plus more as needed

2 frozen bananas

1 frozen kiwi, peeled and chopped

¼ fresh avocado, peeled

½ tsp matcha (see Ingredient Spotlight on page 73)

½ tsp blue-green spirulina (see Ingredient Spotlight on page 54)

2 tbsp (18 g) vanilla or unflavored protein powder

FOR TOPPING

1 kiwi, peeled and sliced

1 tsp hemp seeds (see Ingredient Spotlight on page 77)

½ tsp bee pollen (see Ingredient Spotlight on page 62)

Matcha powder, for dusting (optional)

This recipe combines a ton of green ingredients without including a single leafy-green vegetable. It gets its color and super-nutrient status from kiwi, avocado and both matcha and blue-green spirulina. Matcha provides a slew of natural antioxidants as well as an energy-boosting dose of caffeine and the amino acid L-theanine, while blue-green spirulina adds protein, B vitamins and iron. This bowl has an exceptionally creamy texture thanks to the bananas, avocado and protein powder, along with a uniquely delicious flavor that will leave you satisfied.

Add the almond milk, frozen bananas, frozen kiwi, avocado, matcha, spirulina and protein powder to a blender or food processor. Blend on high, using a tamper tool, if available, to smash down the ingredients and help them blend. Stop and scrape down the sides every so often as needed, adding more almond milk, 1 tablespoon (15 ml) at a time, until it's totally smooth, but still thick.

Transfer the mixture to a bowl, then fan out the kiwi slices on top. Sprinkle with the hemp seeds and bee pollen, dust with the matcha powder if desired, then serve immediately.

Tip: This bowl gets a big boost of protein thanks to the addition of protein powder. You can use whichever kind you prefer, be it whey, hemp, pea or any other variety on the market. An unflavored protein powder will meld seamlessly into the recipe without any additives, while a vanilla protein powder will give it more flavor and sweetness, but will also have additional ingredients. Always read the label to make sure it's something you're comfortable putting in your body.

Pep in Your Step

Makes one bowl

FOR THE BASE
¼ cup (60 ml) coconut milk, plus more as needed

1½ frozen bananas

1 cup (150 g) frozen strawberries

2 tbsp (20 g) frozen raspberries

½ tsp vanilla extract

2 tbsp (18 g) collagen peptides

FOR TOPPING
¼ cup (38 g) Super Seed Granola (page 146)

½ banana, sliced

5 fresh raspberries

This recipe features one of my favorite smoothie bowl add-ins: collagen peptides. In addition to the incredible health benefits of consuming collagen, it also gives this bowl a smooth, creamy texture and doesn't produce a grainy texture like some protein powders do. This bowl gets its tang from raspberries, which have a much stronger flavor than strawberries, so you only need a handful for amazing flavor.

Add the coconut milk, frozen bananas, frozen strawberries, frozen raspberries, vanilla and collagen peptides to a blender or food processor. Blend on high, using a tamper tool, if available, to smash down the ingredients and stopping to scrape down the sides as needed. Blend until the mixture is nice and smooth, adding more coconut milk, 1 tablespoon (15 ml) at a time as needed to get everything moving.

Transfer the mixture to a bowl, then top with the granola. Arrange the banana and raspberries on top, then serve immediately.

Ingredient Spotlight: Collagen. This is the most abundant protein found in the body and contains high levels of the amino acids arginine, glycine, proline and hydroxyproline, among others. Collagen is said to improve the health and vitality of skin, hair, nails, tendons, cartilage, bones, joints and the gut. Collagen peptides are sourced from bovine (cow) hides, and are typically unflavored and not detectable when blended into a smoothie bowl, although this can vary from brand to brand. Choose a reputable brand that sources collagen from grass-fed, pasture-raised bovine hides to ensure a natural, high-quality and neutral-flavored product.

Muscle Monkey

Makes one bowl

FOR THE BASE
¼ cup (60 ml) almond milk, plus more as needed

2 frozen bananas

2 tbsp (30 g) peanut butter

2 tbsp (18 g) vanilla protein powder

FOR TOPPING
2 tbsp (30 ml) Honey Peanut Butter Drizzle (page 165)

½ banana, sliced

1 tbsp (9 g) cacao nibs (see Ingredient Spotlight on page 109)

1 tsp Power Seed Sprinkle (page 149)

Think of this bowl as a healthy version of the ice cream "Chunky Monkey." It's packed with protein and nutrition rather than fat and sugar, so instead of making you chunky, it will help you build muscles.

Vanilla protein powder gives this bowl a serious boost of protein in addition to a rich and creamy flavor that makes it straight-up taste like ice cream. This hunger-satisfying bowl makes an incredible breakfast, meal replacement or ultra-healthy dessert.

Add the almond milk, frozen bananas, peanut butter and protein powder to a blender or food processor. Blend on high, using a tamper tool, if available, to smash down the ingredients and stopping to scrape down the sides as needed. Blend until smooth, adding more almond milk, 1 tablespoon (15 ml) at a time as needed to get everything moving, but try to add as little liquid as possible in order to keep it thick.

Transfer the mixture to a bowl, then swirl in the Honey Peanut Butter Drizzle. Arrange the banana on top, sprinkle with the cacao nibs and Power Seed Sprinkle, then serve immediately.

Tip: Use whichever kind of protein powder you like: whey, hemp, soy, pea or any other variety on the market. If you prefer an unflavored protein powder, it will work fine, but add ¼ teaspoon of vanilla extract to make up for the lost vanilla flavor.

Morning Mango Matcha

Makes one bowl

This lovely avocado-green bowl will leave you satisfied in addition to giving you lots of energy for the day. Matcha has a slightly bitter, earthy flavor that tastes great blended with mango.

FOR THE BASE

¼ cup (60 ml) almond milk, plus more as needed

1 tsp matcha powder

1 frozen banana

1½ cups (225 g) frozen mango

FOR TOPPING

1 tsp Power Seed Sprinkle (page 149)

½ kiwi, peeled and sliced

¼ mango, diced

Edible flower, such as a pansy (optional)

Add the almond milk, matcha powder, frozen banana and frozen mango to a blender or food processor. Blend on high, using a tamper tool, if available, to smash down the ingredients and stopping to scrape down the sides as needed. Blend until smooth, adding more almond milk, 1 tablespoon (15 ml) at a time as needed to help move things around.

Transfer the mixture to a bowl, smooth it out, then dust with the Power Seed Sprinkle. Arrange the kiwi and mango on top, garnish with an edible flower if desired, then serve immediately.

Ingredient Spotlight: Matcha.
This antioxidant-rich Japanese green tea powder has been touted for its slew of nutritional benefits, and many people have started replacing their morning coffee with a matcha latte instead. Matcha is made from green-tea leaves using a special process that extracts more caffeine and L-theanine, which are said to boost mood and brain function when ingested together.

Sneaky Little Veggies

◀ ▲ ▶

Starting each morning with a veggie-packed smoothie bowl is my secret to living a healthy, balanced lifestyle. I can relax knowing that regardless of what else I eat that day, I've still managed to consume plenty of fruits and veggies.

Green smoothies were once considered a crazy health fad, but they've become so mainstream that few people bat an eyelash at them anymore. Practically everyone is putting kale and spinach in their smoothies these days. I love other greens like collards, chard and arugula, but their vegetal taste is much too strong, even when combined with overpowering flavors like peanut butter and banana. So I don't recommend trying them unless you're really into that sort of thing.

There are loads of other vegetables that blend seamlessly into smoothie bowls that don't get nearly enough attention, like frozen cauliflower and zucchini.

If you're trying to incorporate more greens into your diet or attempting to trick a toddler (or husband) into eating the veggies he thinks he hates, this chapter is for you. The recipes in this section span from your basic green bowl to a kid-friendly bowl that tastes just like a PB&J sandwich, and even a few out-of-the box bowls made with frozen peas and corn. Whether you're a vegetable lover or hater doesn't matter. This chapter has a little something for everyone.

Green Head

Makes one bowl

FOR THE BASE

2 tbsp (30 ml) pineapple juice

2 tbsp (30 ml) coconut milk, plus more as needed

1 large handful kale (2-3 leaves with tender stems), torn into pieces

1 frozen banana

1 cup (150 g) frozen pineapple

¼ fresh avocado, peeled

FOR TOPPING

¼ cup (38 g) Classic Granola (page 141)

¼ cup (38 g) pineapple slices or chunks

½ banana, sliced

1 tsp hemp seeds

This bowl is a variation on the Green Head smoothie, which was the very first recipe I created for Soulberri. The smoothie gets its name from a big, pesky green fly that has essentially become our town's mascot.

This bowl is super creamy from the addition of bananas, coconut milk and avocado, but is still light and tangy thanks to the frozen pineapple and pineapple juice. At Soulberri, we blend the hemp seeds in, but for the bowl I opted to add them on top instead. For an extra boost of protein and nutrition, feel free to do both.

Add the pineapple juice, coconut milk, kale, frozen banana, frozen pineapple and avocado to a blender or food processor. Blend on high, stopping to scrape down the sides as needed and using a tamper tool, if available, to help move things around. Blend until totally smooth and there are no remaining bits of kale, adding more coconut milk, 1 tablespoon (15 ml) at a time as needed to get things moving.

Transfer the mixture to a bowl, then top with the granola and arrange the pineapple and banana on top. Sprinkle with hemp seeds and serve immediately.

Ingredient Spotlight: Hemp Seeds. Also known as "hemp hearts," these small, black and tan morsels come from the hemp plant and are packed with fiber, omega-3 fatty acids and complete protein. While they are harvested from a cannabis plant, they are 100% legal and will not get you stoned. They can be added as a topping or blended into a smoothie bowl base.

Peanut Butter & Jelly Surprise

Makes one bowl

FOR THE BASE

¼ cup (60 ml) Concord grape juice, plus more as needed

¾ cup (115 g) frozen strawberries

¾ cup (115 g) frozen grapes

¾ cup (115 g) frozen cauliflower

2 tbsp (30 g) smooth peanut butter

FOR TOPPING

2 tbsp (30 g) Peanut Butter Magic (page 162), divided

¼ cup (38 g) Classic Granola (page 141)

1 tbsp (9 g) chopped salted peanuts

1 small cluster fresh or frozen red grapes

Here's the cool thing about peanut butter—it overpowers just about everything. In this case, it's cauliflower. Surprise! This is an incredible way to get your kids to practically inhale a cruciferous vegetable because they'll never know it's in there (unless you want them to). It tastes just like a frozen version of that old childhood favorite, but with no added sugar and way more nutrition.

There's really no substitute for the Concord grape juice as it's essential for getting that authentic peanut butter and jelly flavor.

Add the Concord grape juice, frozen strawberries, frozen grapes, frozen cauliflower and peanut butter to a blender or food processor. Blend on high, stopping to scrape down the sides every few seconds as needed. If you have a tamper tool, use that to help smash down the ingredients to help them mix easier. Blend until smooth, adding more grape juice, 1 tablespoon (15 ml) at a time, to help facilitate blending.

Transfer half of the smoothie mixture to a bowl, drizzle with 1 tablespoon (15 g) of the Peanut Butter Magic, then pour the rest of the mixture over that and smooth out the top. Drizzle with the remaining tablespoon (15 g) of the Peanut Butter Magic, then place in the freezer for 30 seconds to firm up the magic. Sprinkle with the granola, then garnish with chopped peanuts and grapes. Serve immediately.

Strawberry Lime Zucchini Basil

Makes one bowl

You'll be hard pressed to find any signs of zucchini while eating this bowl, even though there's an entire cup of it. The flavor screams summer, with an intense fruit-forward taste, sorbet-like texture and herbal basil scent in the background. I like to keep the toppings minimal in order to let the flavorful blend shine. If you know anyone who cringes at the mere thought of eating a plate of steamed summer squash, make them this bowl and watch their opinion of this versatile veggie change right before your eyes.

FOR THE BASE
¼ cup (60 ml) apple juice, plus more as needed

2 tsp (10 ml) fresh lime juice

1 tsp fresh lime zest

2 cups (300 g) frozen strawberries

1 cup (150 g) frozen zucchini

¼ cup (6 g) loosely packed fresh basil leaves

FOR TOPPING
2–3 strawberries, sliced

Sprig of basil, for garnish (optional)

Lime wheel, for garnish (optional)

Add the apple juice, lime juice, lime zest, frozen strawberries, frozen zucchini and basil leaves to a blender or food processor. Blend on high, scraping down the sides as needed until totally smooth. If the mixture is not blending well, add more apple juice in small amounts just to get it moving, but be careful not to add too much or the mixture will be watery.

Transfer the mixture to a bowl, then arrange the strawberry slices on top. Garnish with the basil sprig and lime wheel if desired, then serve immediately.

Tip: Look for frozen sliced zucchini in the frozen veggie section of your grocery store, or freeze it yourself.

Piña Caul-lada

Makes one bowl

This bowl looks and tastes just like a piña colada, only it's hiding an entire cup (150 g) of cauliflower inside. I modernized this classic tropical drink by turning it into a bowl and squeezing in some healthy, cruciferous veggies. By taking out the booze and sugar and replacing them with a healthy veggie instead, this recipe has been completely transformed to be as good for you as it tastes—and it tastes like a day on the beach! This bowl will instantly make you feel like you're basking in the tropics no matter what it looks like outside your window.

FOR THE BASE

¼ cup (60 ml) full-fat canned coconut milk, plus more as needed

1 tbsp (15 ml) honey or agave nectar

2 cups (300 g) frozen pineapple

1 cup (150 g) frozen cauliflower

FOR TOPPING

2 tbsp (30 ml) Coconut Whipped Cream (page 157)

¼ cup (38 g) fresh pineapple chunks

1 tbsp (9 g) unsweetened coconut flakes

Add the coconut milk, honey, frozen pineapple and frozen cauliflower to a blender or food processor. Blend on high, using a tamper tool, if available, to smash down the ingredients and stopping to scrape down the sides as needed. Blend until the mixture is totally smooth, adding more coconut milk, 1 tablespoon (15 ml) at a time as needed to get everything moving.

Transfer the mixture to a bowl, smooth out the top, then dollop with the Coconut Whipped Cream. Arrange the pineapple chunks on top, sprinkle with the coconut flakes, then serve immediately.

Jalapeño Honeydew Mint

Makes one bowl

FOR THE BASE

¼ cup (60 ml) white grape juice, plus more as needed

2 tsp (10 ml) fresh lime or lemon juice

2½ cups (375 g) frozen honeydew chunks

2-4 thin slices jalapeño pepper, more or less to taste, seeds removed for less heat

¼ avocado, peeled

¼ cup (6 g) loosely packed fresh mint leaves

FOR TOPPING

¼ cup (45 g) sliced fresh honeydew melon

3-4 very thin slices jalapeño pepper

4-5 fresh mint leaves

This frosty, pale-green bowl is a uniquely refreshing treat on a hot summer day. The jalapeño adds complexity and just a touch of heat, but if you're really opposed to spicy foods you can leave it out. This bowl will still taste great without it, as the mint provides an additional boost of flavor. Avocado lends a creamy element, while a spritz of lemon or lime juice wakes the whole thing up.

For best results, save this recipe for the middle to end of summer when melons are at their peak. A ripe, in-season melon should provide enough sweetness, but if you find it to be lacking, feel free to add a touch of honey or agave nectar.

Add the white grape juice, lemon or lime juice, frozen honeydew, jalapeño slices, avocado and mint leaves to a blender or food processor. Blend on high, scraping down the sides as needed until totally smooth. If the mixture is not blending well, add more grape juice in small amounts just to get it moving, but be careful not to add too much or the mixture will be too watery. If you have a tamper tool available, use that to help facilitate blending.

Spoon the mixture into a bowl and smooth out the top. Fan out the honeydew slices and arrange them on top, then place the jalapeño slices and mint leaves all around. Serve immediately.

Tip: Jalapeños, like all chiles, can vary widely in their heat level. Sometimes even the tiniest bit will set your mouth on fire, while other times they're as mild as a bell pepper. Taste a small amount of the pepper prior to adding it to the blender so you know what you're working with.

Tahini Beetkini

Makes one bowl

FOR THE BASE

¼ cup (60 ml) freshly squeezed orange juice, plus more as needed

½ tsp orange zest

1 frozen banana

1½ cups (225 g) frozen red grapes

¼ cup (40 g) cooked red beets, chopped

FOR TOPPING

2 tbsp (30 ml) Tahini Maple Drizzle (page 166)

5 orange segments

2 tbsp (20 g) crumbled Bird Seed Brittle (page 150)

Beet lovers rejoice! Beet haters, move along. The thing with beets is they have a hard time being sneaky—their earthy taste peeks through, even with the other strong flavors in this bowl like banana, orange and tahini. If you love beets, however, that should be music to your ears.

Beets and tahini are an awesome combination in savory food, and they work together equally well in this bowl. Beets also pair beautifully with orange, so here I use a splash of OJ along with a touch of orange zest to really marry the flavors together.

This bowl has a slight, but delightfully bitter taste from the tahini, which goes exceptionally well with the sweet beets and Bird Seed Brittle (page 150). The brittle adds the most wonderful salty caramel crunch that plays against the other ingredients brilliantly. It's worth the extra effort to make this topping, and the leftovers are great for snacking.

Add the orange juice, orange zest, frozen banana, frozen grapes and beets to a blender or food processor. Blend on high, stopping every few seconds to scrape down the sides using a tamper tool (if available) to smash down the ingredients and move things around. Blend until the mixture is nice and smooth, like sorbet, adding more orange juice, 1 tablespoon (15 ml) at a time as needed.

Transfer the mixture to a bowl, then drizzle with the Tahini Maple Drizzle. Arrange the orange segments like flower petals around the perimeter of the bowl, sprinkle with the Bird Seed Brittle and serve immediately.

Mermaid Bubbles

Makes one bowl

This fun and whimsical bowl is an extra veggie-packed version of the Magical Mermaid bowl (page 54). I've not only added spinach and blue-green spirulina for that deep ocean-green color, but also zucchini, which adds creaminess as well as an extra serving of veggies. This bowl has a uniquely sweet flavor that masks the taste of the veggies and has a real show-stopping presentation.

FOR THE BASE

¼ cup (60 ml) coconut milk, plus more as needed

¼ tsp vanilla extract

1½ frozen bananas

½ cup (75 g) frozen zucchini

½ cup (75 g) frozen honeydew melon

½ cup (12 g) loosely packed baby spinach

¼ tsp blue-green spirulina (see Ingredient Spotlight on page 54)

FOR TOPPING

1 tbsp (3 g) puffed millet (see Ingredient Spotlight on page 125)

1 tsp unsweetened coconut flakes

¼ cup (38 g) honeydew melon balls in various sizes

¼ cup (38 g) white pitaya (dragon fruit) balls in various sizes (see Pro Styling Tip on page 26)

Add the coconut milk, vanilla, frozen bananas, frozen zucchini, frozen honeydew, spinach and spirulina to a blender or food processor. Blend on high, using a tamper tool, if available, to smash down the ingredients and stopping to scrape down the sides every so often as needed. Blend until the mixture is smooth and creamy, adding more coconut milk, 1 tablespoon (15 ml) at a time as needed, just to help get everything moving.

Transfer the mixture to a bowl, then sprinkle with the puffed millet and coconut flakes. Artfully arrange the honeydew and dragon fruit balls in a random pattern along one side of the bowl, then serve immediately.

Pro Styling Tip: Use a melon baller to scoop out the flesh of the fruit in order to achieve the bubble-like appearance on top. You can use different sized melon ballers to create a more varied appearance, like in the photo, but using all one size will still get the point across. A sharp-edged measuring spoon can also produce good results.

Ginger Cauli Melba

Makes one bowl

Here we have a super-healthy twist on Peach Melba, the classic dessert made of peaches and raspberry sauce. I like to sneak cauliflower into this smoothie bowl to give it a virtually tasteless boost of fiber and nutrients. The tart raspberries and sweet peaches along with a spicy hit of ginger make the cauliflower go completely unnoticed.

FOR THE BASE
¼ cup (60 ml) apple juice, plus more as needed

2 tbsp (20 g) frozen raspberries

2 cups (300 g) frozen peaches

½ cup (75 g) frozen cauliflower

½ tsp freshly grated ginger

FOR TOPPING
5 peach slices

5 fresh raspberries

1 tbsp (9 g) sliced or slivered almonds

Add the apple juice, frozen raspberries, frozen peaches, frozen cauliflower and ginger to a blender or food processor. Blend on high, using a tamper tool, if available, to smash down the ingredients and stopping to scrape down the sides as needed. Blend until the mixture is as smooth as sorbet, adding more apple juice, 1 tablespoon (15 ml) at a time, to help facilitate blending.

Transfer the mixture to a bowl, smooth it out, then arrange the sliced peaches and raspberries on top. Sprinkle with the sliced almonds and serve immediately.

Tip: Be sure to finely grate the ginger on a microplane, as its long fibers can give your blender a run for its money.

Sweet Pea & Mint

Makes one bowl

FOR THE BASE
¼ cup (60 ml) coconut milk, plus more as needed

1¾ frozen bananas

¾ cup (115 g) frozen peas

¼ cup (6 g) loosely packed fresh mint leaves

FOR TOPPING
1 tbsp (9 g) unsweetened coconut flakes

1 tbsp (3 g) puffed millet (see Ingredient Spotlight on page 125)

4-5 fresh mint leaves

One of the most popular plant-based protein powders on the market is pea protein because it has a clean flavor and smooth texture when blended into smoothies and smoothie bowls. Here, I've taken peas in their pure form to create a bowl that's inspired by the classic cold English pea and mint soup. Not only do the peas give a boost of protein and fiber, but they also add natural sweetness. This bowl is as unique as it is refreshing and especially lovely when enjoyed in the spring.

Add the coconut milk, frozen bananas, frozen peas and mint to a blender or food processor. Blend on high, stopping to scrape down the sides as needed. If available, use a tamper tool to help work the ingredients around. Blend until smooth, adding more coconut milk, 1 tablespoon (15 ml) at a time as needed, just to get things moving.

Transfer the mixture to a bowl, then smooth out the top. Sprinkle with the coconut flakes and puffed millet. Garnish with the mint leaves and serve immediately.

Tip: Store-bought frozen peas are ideal to use here. They're not only inexpensive and easy to find, they're always picked and packaged at peak ripeness, so they're sweeter and not as starchy as they can sometimes be when fresh.

Sweet Potato Pecan

Makes one bowl

FOR THE BASE

¼ cup (60 ml) freshly squeezed orange juice, plus more as needed

¼ tsp orange zest

1½ frozen bananas

1 cup (200 g) cooked, mashed sweet potatoes (peeled)

1 date, soaked in hot water for 10 minutes, then drained

¼ tsp vanilla extract

¼ tsp cinnamon

Pinch of salt

FOR TOPPING

2 tbsp (30 ml) Vanilla Cashew Butter Drizzle (page 165)

6 whole raw pecans

Cinnamon, for dusting

This is a riff on one of my favorite Thanksgiving side dishes: mashed sweet potatoes with lots of butter and brown sugar, scented with orange and topped with crunchy pecans. I've taken those flavors and turned them into a smoothie bowl instead, so it has a frosty consistency, loads more nutrition and no added sugar or butter.

Dates provide a sweet caramel flavor that mimics brown sugar, while orange juice and zest really pack a punch. On its own, this blend has a strong flavor from the orange and cinnamon, but the Vanilla Cashew Butter Drizzle (page 165) really balances the whole thing out, so don't skip it!

Add the orange juice, orange zest, frozen bananas, sweet potatoes, date, vanilla, cinnamon and salt to a blender or food processor. Blend on high, stopping to scrape down the sides as needed and using a tamper tool, if available, to smash down the ingredients and move them around. Blend until smooth, adding more orange juice, 1 tablespoon (15 ml) at a time as needed to get everything moving.

Transfer the mixture to a bowl, then drizzle with the Vanilla Cashew Butter Drizzle. Arrange the pecans in a circle, dust with the cinnamon and serve immediately.

Stealthy Healthy Açaí

Makes one bowl

FOR THE BASE

¼ cup (60 ml) apple juice, plus more as needed

1 (3.5-oz [100-g]) frozen packet unsweetened açaí purée (see Ingredient Spotlight on page 13)

½ cup (75 g) frozen red seedless grapes

½ frozen banana

½ cup (75 g) frozen cauliflower

FOR TOPPING

¼ cup (38 g) Super Seed Granola (page 146)

½ banana, sliced

2–3 fresh strawberries, sliced

¼ cup (38 g) fresh blueberries

2 tbsp (30 g) almond butter

1 tbsp (15 ml) honey, or more or less to taste

This is like the Classic Açaí bowl (page 13), but with some secret veggies hiding beneath the surface. This recipe sneaks in a half cup (75 g) of frozen cauliflower, but it's impossible to notice the flavor as it melds seamlessly into the blend. I've also upped the health factor by swapping out the Classic Granola for the Super Seed Granola (page 146) and added even more fruit and a protein-packed dollop of almond butter on top. Consider this the Classic Açaí bowl on steroids.

Add the apple juice to a blender or food processor. Break up the açaí packet into a few smaller pieces, then add it to the blender along with the frozen grapes, frozen banana and frozen cauliflower. Blend on high, stopping to scrape down the sides every so often as needed. If available, use a tamper tool to help work the ingredients around. Blend until smooth, adding more apple juice, 1 tablespoon (15 ml) at a time as needed, just to get things moving.

Transfer the mixture to a bowl, then sprinkle with the granola. Fan out the banana slices on one side of the bowl, along with the strawberries and blueberries. Drizzle with the almond butter and honey, then serve immediately.

Fennel Orange Apricot

Makes one bowl

FOR THE BASE

1 medium orange, peeled, seeds and pith removed

¼ tsp orange zest

2 cups (300 g) frozen sliced apricots (about 4 apricots)

¼ small fennel bulb, core removed, roughly chopped

1 tbsp (15 ml) honey

Orange juice, if needed

FOR TOPPING

½ sliced apricot (substitute dried apricots if unavailable)

3 small orange slices

2 tbsp (19 g) Sweet Dukkah (page 153) or fennel pollen

Fennel and orange is a classic combination that you can find in dishes across Italy. A crisp fennel and orange salad is one of my favorite ways to enjoy a light and refreshing meal in the winter, and surprisingly, it tastes just as good in a smoothie bowl. I've additionally paired this recipe with apricots to give it not only sweetness, but a beautiful fruity flavor and smooth texture that truly complements the rest of the bowl.

Add the orange, orange zest, frozen apricots, fennel and honey to a blender or food processor. Blend on high, using a tamper tool, if available, to smash down the ingredients and stopping to scrape down the sides as needed. Blend all of the ingredients until the mixture is nice and smooth, adding orange juice, 1 tablespoon (15 ml) at a time as needed to get everything moving.

Transfer the mixture to a bowl, smooth out the top, then arrange the apricots and orange slices on top. Sprinkle with the Sweet Dukkah, then serve immediately.

Tips: Since this recipe uses a whole, fresh orange, there is no need for additional liquid. However, if your blender is struggling to break down the frozen fruit, you can add more orange juice a little bit at a time to help things get moving.

Apricots are not commonly found frozen, but they're fairly easy to freeze yourself since they don't need to be peeled. Slice in half, remove the pit, then slice and arrange on a parchment-lined sheet pan in an even layer. Freeze until solid, then transfer to a ziplock bag for longer storage.

Pineapple Cucumber Cilantro Avocado

Makes one bowl

FOR THE BASE
⅓ cup (50 g) cucumber slices, peeled and seeded

1 frozen banana

1 cup (150 g) frozen pineapple

¼ avocado, peeled

2 tbsp (3 g) roughly chopped fresh cilantro

Pineapple juice, only if needed

FOR TOPPING
¼ cup (38 g) sliced pineapple

1-2 pineapple flowers, for garnish (page 167) (optional)

Sprig of cilantro, for garnish (optional)

This recipe was inspired by a winter trip to Tulum, Mexico, where I came down with a nasty cold. Instead of drinking margaritas all day in the sun, I was opting for glass after glass of ice-cold, ultra-hydrating, nonalcoholic agua fresca instead. These Mexican fruit-infused drinks are so refreshing on a hot day, and my favorite one from that trip combined pineapple, cucumber and fresh cilantro. Here I've added some avocado for creaminess and just a tiny bit of banana for texture and added sweetness. This bowl is on the less-sweet side, but I find it to be incredibly cool and satisfying.

Add the cucumber, frozen banana, frozen pineapple, avocado and cilantro to a blender or food processor. Blend on high, using a tamper tool, if available, to smash down the ingredients, stopping to scrape down the sides as needed. Blend until the mixture is smooth, but if you need to add a bit more liquid to help things move, you can add pineapple juice, 1 tablespoon (15 ml) at a time. Be sure to add as little liquid as possible in order to achieve a nice thick texture.

Transfer the mixture to a bowl, then arrange the pineapple slices on top. Garnish with a pineapple flower and sprig of cilantro, then serve immediately.

Tip: Because this recipe calls for fresh cucumber, not frozen, it should provide enough liquid for blending. If you're still having trouble getting the ingredients to break down, you can add pineapple juice a little bit at a time to help get things moving. You can also opt to use plain old water, but it will dilute the flavors a bit.

Sweet Corn Caramel

Makes one bowl

FOR THE BASE

¼ cup (60 ml) coconut milk, plus more as needed

2 frozen bananas

½ cup (75 g) frozen corn

Pinch of sea salt

¼ tsp pure vanilla extract

FOR TOPPING

1 tbsp (15 ml) Salted Date Caramel Sauce (page 158)

¼ cup (3 g) lightly salted popcorn (store-bought is fine)

2 tsp (6 g) sunflower seeds

With sweet frozen corn blended with banana, vanilla and sea salt for a unique flavor, this smoothie bowl is unlike any you've ever had before. I love it topped with lightly salted popcorn for a crunchy and unexpected textural contrast. This bowl was inspired by two things: the caramel popcorn I grew up eating and my friend Veronica. She grew up in Ecuador and finishes her famous shrimp ceviche with a mound of salty popcorn, which is what gave me the idea to do the same on this bowl.

The play of savory saltiness against the sweet date caramel is a familiar flavor, yet served in an unexpected way that's bound to make your mouth water.

Add the coconut milk, frozen bananas, frozen corn, sea salt and vanilla to a blender or food processor. Blend on high, stopping to scrape down the sides every so often and using a tamper tool, if available, to smash down the ingredients. Add more coconut milk, 1 tablespoon (15 ml) at a time, to help get everything moving, but only if absolutely needed. Blend until the mixture is nice and smooth, but know that there will still be some texture from the corn.

Transfer the mixture to a bowl, then smooth out the top. Drizzle with the Salted Date Caramel Sauce, top with the popcorn and sunflower seeds and serve immediately.

Carrot Cake

Makes one bowl

Even most veggie haters can't deny the charm of a well-made carrot cake, as the carrots meld beautifully into the sweet batter. But if we're being honest with ourselves, the real appeal of a carrot cake has nothing to do with the cake itself, it's all about the cream-cheese frosting. Vanilla Greek yogurt gets blended in to give a cream cheese–like flavor to this recipe, while the Vanilla Cashew Butter Drizzle (page 165) acts as an icing of sorts. The walnuts and coconut flakes give it great textural contrast in addition to added fiber and healthy fats.

FOR THE BASE

¼ cup (60 ml) almond milk, plus more as needed

1 frozen banana

¼ cup (38 g) frozen pineapple

1 cup (150 g) diced fresh carrots (from about 2 medium carrots)

½ cup (125 g) vanilla Greek yogurt

1 tbsp (15 ml) maple syrup

¼ tsp cinnamon

Pinch of salt

FOR TOPPING

1 tbsp (9 g) chopped walnuts

1 tsp unsweetened coconut flakes

1 tbsp (15 ml) Vanilla Cashew Butter Drizzle (page 165)

Dried Pineapple Flower (page 167) (optional)

1 blueberry (optional)

Add the almond milk, frozen banana, frozen pineapple, carrots, yogurt, maple syrup, cinnamon and a pinch of salt to a blender or food processor. Blend on high, stopping to scrape down the sides every so often as needed. If available, use a tamper tool to smash down the ingredients in order to get them moving. Blend until the mixture is nice and smooth, adding more almond milk, 1 tablespoon (15 ml) at a time, to help facilitate blending.

Transfer the mixture to a bowl, then sprinkle with the walnuts and coconut flakes. Drizzle with the Vanilla Cashew Butter Drizzle, garnish with a Dried Pineapple Flower with the blueberry in the center if desired, then serve immediately.

Tip: For a dairy-free version, swap out the yogurt for your favorite nondairy yogurt.

We All Scream For Nice Cream

◀▲▶

I love cookies, cakes, pies—really, anything sweet—but my all-time favorite treat is ice cream. I've never been a person to stick to a strict diet, but there has to be a balance between the foods that feed your body with nutrients, and the foods that fill your soul with joy. This chapter celebrates both.

The term "nice cream" was coined to describe a frozen blended treat that has the same texture and appeal as ice cream, only it's made without any dairy or refined sugar, and instead relies on the magic of puréed frozen fruit. When blended, frozen bananas take on an ethereal quality. Their sweetness is heightened, their banana flavor is mellowed, and they develop a velvety texture.

When most people try a basic "nice cream" for the first time, they're often blown away by how good it tastes. Even those who scoff at the idea of a "healthy" dessert are pleasantly surprised by how delicious it really is. The rich, substantial bowls in this chapter are perfect for splitting with a friend, especially if you're choosing to enjoy them for dessert.

Mint Chocolate Chip

Makes one bowl

FOR THE BASE

¼ cup (60 ml) coconut milk, plus more as needed

⅛ tsp spearmint extract

2½ frozen bananas

¼ tsp blue-green spirulina (see Ingredient Spotlight on page 54)

¼ cup (6 g) loosely packed fresh mint leaves

2 tbsp (30 ml) Chocolate Magic (page 162)

FOR TOPPING

1 tbsp (9 g) cacao nibs

Mint sprig, for garnish

Ingredient Spotlight: Cacao Nibs. These are

the raw, broken-up bits of cacao beans that have been dried and fermented for flavor. They are intensely chocolaty, unsweetened and have a nice bite to them. Since they're minimally processed, they contain high amounts of antioxidants and other trace nutrients.

Mint chocolate chip is one of the most popular ice cream flavors out there. It's sweet and creamy, cool and refreshing, and has tasty bits of dark chocolate studded throughout. What's not to love? This recipe combines frozen bananas with fresh mint and spearmint extract to create a super minty base, along with a touch of spirulina to get that unmistakable pale green hue.

Add the coconut milk, spearmint extract, frozen bananas, spirulina and fresh mint to a blender or food processor. Blend on high, stopping to scrape down the sides every so often as needed and using a tamper tool, if available, to help facilitate blending. Blend until the mixture is smooth like ice cream, adding more coconut milk, 1 tablespoon (15 ml) at a time, only if absolutely needed, in order to keep the mixture as thick as possible.

When the mixture is smooth, drizzle the Chocolate Magic into the blender, then pulse a few times on low speed until the Chocolate Magic breaks up to form tiny "chips." Be careful not to overmix at this point or your chips will blend into the mixture.

Transfer the mixture to a bowl, then sprinkle with the cacao nibs. Garnish with a sprig of mint and serve immediately.

Tip: It's important to use spearmint extract here instead of peppermint. Spearmint is milder and sweeter, making it perfect for applications like this. Search for it online, or omit altogether and double up on the fresh mint leaves instead.

Chocolate Peanut Butter Cup

Makes one bowl

FOR THE BASE

¼ cup (60 ml) coconut milk, plus more as needed

¼ tsp vanilla extract

2 frozen bananas

2 (1-oz [30-ml]) coconut milk ice cubes (see tutorial on page 9)

3 tbsp (45 g) peanut butter

1 tbsp (15 ml) honey

FOR TOPPING

2 tbsp (30 ml) Chocolate Magic (page 162), divided

2 tbsp (30 ml) Peanut Butter Magic (page 162), divided

1 tbsp (9 g) chopped roasted, salted peanuts

This is the healthiest version of a peanut butter cup you'll ever try! Made with a base of frozen bananas, coconut milk, peanut butter, honey and vanilla, it tastes like a creamy dreamy peanut butter ice cream. It's so good, you could eat it on its own and be totally satisfied, but for it to be a true peanut butter cup it needs some chocolate. Homemade Chocolate Magic (page 162) is just the thing to add that smooth, melt-in-your-mouth chocolaty layer. For a little crunch, I like to add some salty chopped peanuts on top as well. You can totally use unsalted if you like, but I find that little bit of salt up against the sweet base makes this bowl seriously addictive.

Add the coconut milk, vanilla, frozen bananas, coconut milk ice cubes, peanut butter and honey to a blender or food processor. Blend on high, stopping to scrape down the sides as needed. If you have a tamper tool, use it to help mash down the ingredients and mix them around. Blend until smooth, adding more coconut milk, 1 tablespoon (15 ml) at a time, as needed.

Transfer half of the mixture to a bowl, then drizzle with 1 tablespoon (15 ml) of the Chocolate Magic and 1 tablespoon (15 ml) of the Peanut Butter Magic. Top with the remaining smoothie mixture, then drizzle with the remaining tablespoon (15 ml) each of Chocolate and Peanut Butter Magic. Place in the freezer to allow the magic to set up for 30 seconds, sprinkle with the chopped peanuts, then serve immediately.

Key Lime Pie

Makes one bowl

Makes one bowl

FOR THE BASE

2 tbsp (30 ml) coconut milk, plus more as needed

2 tbsp (30 ml) fresh lime juice

1 tsp lime zest

4 (1-oz [30-ml]) coconut milk ice cubes (see tutorial on page 9)

1½ frozen bananas

¼ avocado, peeled

2 tbsp (30 ml) honey or agave nectar

¼ tsp vanilla extract

⅛ tsp blue-green spirulina (see Ingredient Spotlight on page 54)

FOR TOPPING

¼ cup (38 g) Classic Granola (page 141)

2 tbsp (30 ml) Coconut Whipped Cream (page 157)

Lime zest, for garnish (optional)

Tiny lime slice, for garnish (optional)

I love Key lime pie, but it can often taste too cloyingly sweet. This version is not only healthier, but is ultra creamy, tangy and just sweet enough. Avocado is added for richness and also a cool green color, which is further heightened by just a touch of blue-green spirulina. Plenty of fresh lime juice and lime zest really drive home that iconic sour flavor, while honey adds just a touch of sweetness for balance without going overboard.

Crunchy granola mimics the signature graham cracker crust, while Coconut Whipped Cream (page 157) adds the finishing touch. This smoothie bowl tastes just like a frozen Key lime pie, only made with healthy, whole-food ingredients. Win!

Add the coconut milk, lime juice, lime zest, coconut milk ice cubes, frozen bananas, avocado, honey or agave nectar, vanilla and spirulina to a blender or food processor. Blend on high until the mixture is smooth and creamy. If you have a tamper tool available, use it to smash down the ingredients in order to help facilitate blending. Stop to scrape down the sides every so often, and if needed, add more coconut milk, 1 tablespoon (15 ml) at a time, to achieve a thick, creamy consistency.

Transfer the mixture to a bowl, sprinkle with the Classic Granola, then dollop the Coconut Whipped Cream on top. Garnish with the lime zest and tiny lime slice if desired, then serve immediately.

Pro Styling Tip: Sprinkle granola around the perimeter of the bowl and place whipped cream in the center to mimic the appearance of a pie.

Cookies & Cream

FOR THE BASE

¼ cup (60 ml) coconut milk, plus more as needed

¼ tsp vanilla extract

4 (1-oz [30-ml]) coconut milk ice cubes (see tutorial on page 9)

1½ frozen bananas

1 tbsp (15 ml) maple syrup

Pinch of salt

2 tbsp (30 ml) Chocolate Magic (page 162)

FOR TOPPING

¼ cup (38 g) Chocolate Almond Granola (page 142)

2 tbsp (30 ml) Vegan Dark Chocolate Sauce (page 154)

Tip: If you don't want to bother making the Chocolate Magic topping, store-bought mini chocolate chips can be used in a pinch, or even cacao nibs for a less-sweet, ultra-chocolaty version.

Cookies and cream is one of my favorite ice cream flavors, so I wanted to create a "nice cream" version that satisfied just the same. The chocolate "cookie" pieces are made using Chocolate Magic (page 162), which is added to the blend after creating a smooth mixture, and then pulsed on low speed to create the tiny bits that act as the cookie pieces. I use the same technique for the Mint Chocolate Chip bowl (page 109) to mimic the chips. Here, a healthy dose of Chocolate Almond Granola (page 142) makes up for the starchy cookie texture. The addition of Vegan Dark Chocolate Sauce (page 154) is a little bit over the top, but it really makes this bowl look, taste and feel like dessert.

Add the coconut milk, vanilla, coconut milk ice cubes, frozen bananas, maple syrup and salt to a blender or food processor. Blend on high, stopping to scrape down the sides every so often as needed. If you have a tamper tool available, use that to smash down the ingredients and help move everything around. Blend until the mixture is smooth like ice cream. If needed, add more coconut milk, 1 tablespoon (15 ml) at a time, to help blend, but try to add as little liquid as possible in order to achieve a thick consistency.

When the mixture is smooth, drizzle the Chocolate Magic into the blender, then pulse a few times on low speed until it breaks up into little bits.

Transfer the mixture to a bowl, sprinkle with the Chocolate Almond Granola, drizzle with the Vegan Dark Chocolate Sauce, then serve immediately.

Bananas Foster

FOR THE CARAMELIZED BANANAS

2 tsp (10 ml) coconut oil

3 ripe bananas (yellow with some spots)

FOR THE BANANA TOPPING

1 tsp coconut oil

½ banana

FOR THE SMOOTHIE BASE

¼ cup (60 ml) coconut milk, plus more as needed

1 tsp dark rum or ⅛ tsp rum extract

1 date, soaked in hot water for 10 minutes, then drained

Pinch of sea salt

½ tsp cinnamon

FOR THE SMOOTHIE TOPPING

1 tbsp (15 ml) Salted Date Caramel Sauce (page 158)

Cinnamon, for dusting

1 tbsp (9 g) chopped pecans

This recipe is rich, creamy and has a mild kick from dark rum. It doesn't taste boozy by any means, but the rum gives it that iconic Bananas Foster flavor. If you're opposed to using alcohol, you can use a rum extract.

The caramelized bananas are what really set this bowl apart from the rest. Most bowls use raw banana only, but the browned, caramelized fruit gives this smoothie bowl an unmistakable flavor.

Melt the coconut oil in a medium sauté pan over medium heat. Slice the bananas in half lengthwise (they don't need to stay intact), then place them cut-side down in the pan. Cook until they are deep golden brown and caramelized, about 3 to 4 minutes, then flip and cook them on the other side. Remove the bananas to a parchment-lined plate or sheet pan, then freeze until solid, at least 4 hours, but overnight is best.

Right before you're ready to blend, make the topping. Melt the coconut oil in a sauté pan over medium heat. Slice the banana in half lengthwise, then place cut-side down in the pan and cook until deep golden brown and caramelized. Remove from the pan and let cool with the cut side facing up.

Add the coconut milk, rum, frozen caramelized bananas, date, salt and cinnamon to a blender or food processor. Blend on high, stopping to scrape down the sides as needed. If a tamper tool is available, use it to smash down the ingredients and move them around to help facilitate blending. Blend until the mixture is as smooth as ice cream, adding more coconut milk, 1 tablespoon (15 ml) at a time, only if absolutely needed.

Transfer the mixture to a bowl, then arrange the caramelized banana topping on top. Drizzle with the Salted Date Caramel Sauce, dust with the cinnamon, sprinkle with the chopped pecans, then serve immediately.

Chocolate Hazelnut

FOR THE BASE

¼ cup (60 ml) almond milk, plus more as needed

2 frozen bananas

2 (1-oz [30-ml]) almond milk ice cubes (see tutorial on page 9)

3 tbsp (45 g) Chocolate Hazelnut Butter (page 161)

2 tsp (6 g) cacao or good-quality cocoa powder (see Ingredient Spotlight on page 154)

Pinch of salt

FOR TOPPING

2 tbsp (30 g) Chocolate Hazelnut Butter (page 161)

1 tbsp (11 g) chopped toasted hazelnuts

Chocolate and hazelnut is an iconic flavor combination that works fabulously in a smoothie bowl. Frozen bananas and almond milk ice cubes make up the base along with chocolate hazelnut butter and a tiny pinch of salt to bring out the flavors and make this bowl taste absolutely irresistible.

I finish this bowl with a drizzle of Chocolate Hazelnut Butter (page 161) and more chopped roasted hazelnuts for added crunch. You can opt to use a store-bought chocolate hazelnut butter for both the base and the topping, but the homemade version is so much better, and worth the extra effort.

Add the almond milk, frozen bananas, almond milk ice cubes, Chocolate Hazelnut Butter, cacao powder and salt to a blender or food processor. Blend on high, using a tamper tool, if available, to smash down the ingredients, stopping to scrape down the sides as needed. Blend until smooth, adding more almond milk, 1 tablespoon (15 ml) at a time as needed just to get things moving.

Transfer the mixture to a bowl, then swirl in the Chocolate Hazelnut Butter. Sprinkle with the chopped hazelnuts, then serve immediately.

Lemon Chiffon

FOR THE BASE

3 tbsp (45 ml) coconut milk, plus more as needed

2 tbsp (30 ml) fresh lemon juice

1 tsp lemon zest

4 (1-oz [30-ml]) coconut milk ice cubes (see tutorial on page 9)

2 cups (300 g) frozen pineapple

1 tbsp (15 ml) agave nectar

FOR TOPPING

2 tbsp (30 ml) Coconut Whipped Cream (page 157)

1 tbsp (3 g) puffed millet (see Ingredient Spotlight on page 125)

2-3 candied lemon slices (store-bought)

Lemon blossoms or other edible flowers (optional)

Lemon is my all-time favorite fruit because it's so versatile. Making a lemon smoothie bowl wasn't the easiest feat to pull off, but I really wanted to do it and was pleasantly surprised with the result. This recipe uses coconut milk and pineapple as a base, which provides creaminess, acidity, sweetness and a mellow yellow color. It gets its intense lemony flavor from plenty of fresh lemon juice and lemon zest. I use agave nectar to sweeten it because it has a more neutral flavor than honey or maple, but those can absolutely be substituted if you prefer. This bowl is topped with a big dollop of Coconut Whipped Cream (page 157), which cuts the bright acidity of the lemon nicely.

Add the coconut milk, lemon juice, lemon zest, coconut milk ice cubes, frozen pineapple and agave nectar to a blender or food processor. Blend on high, using a tamper tool, if available, to smash down the ingredients, stopping to scrape down the sides every so often. Blend until the mixture is nice and smooth, adding more coconut milk, 1 tablespoon (15 ml) at a time, only if needed to help move things along.

Transfer the mixture to a bowl, smooth out the top, then spoon the Coconut Whipped Cream in the center. Sprinkle with the puffed millet, garnish with the candied lemon slices and edible flowers if desired, then serve immediately.

Tip: Candied lemon slices can be purchased in the dried fruit section of some grocery stores and online. They are more for presentation than flavor, so they can be omitted or swapped out for a few fresh lemon slices instead—just remove the fresh lemon prior to eating.

Caramel Apple Crisp

FOR THE BASE

¼ cup (60 ml) almond milk, plus more as needed

½ frozen banana

2 cups (300 g) frozen peeled apple chunks

½ tsp cinnamon

Pinch of salt

FOR TOPPING

¼ cup (38 g) Cinnamon Pecan Granola (page 145)

¼ apple, cored and thinly sliced

Cinnamon, for dusting

1 tbsp (15 ml) Salted Date Caramel Sauce (page 158)

My family has always been big on apple pie. My grandma taught my mom, who then taught me how to make her signature crust and simple, fruit-forward filling. My husband's family, however, is all about apple crisp. My mother-in-law, Karen, makes the best apple crisp ever, and this is my tribute to her in smoothie-bowl form. Cinnamon Pecan Granola (page 145) mimics the buttery crisp topping without any of the added butter or refined sugar. The frozen base is creamy and smooth with a discernible apple-cinnamon flavor, while cinnamon-dusted apples on top give a bit of textural contrast and a swipe of Salted Date Caramel Sauce (page 158) makes this bowl taste unmistakably like dessert.

Add the almond milk, frozen banana, frozen apples, cinnamon and salt to a blender or food processor. Blend on high, using a tamper tool, if available, to smash down the ingredients and move them around. Stop to scrape down the sides every few minutes as needed, and if things aren't blending easily, add more almond milk, 1 tablespoon (15 ml) at a time, until things start to blend. Be careful not to add too much liquid in order to keep the mixture nice and thick.

Transfer the mixture to a bowl, sprinkle with the Cinnamon Pecan Granola, then fan out the apple slices and dust with a pinch of cinnamon. Drizzle with the Salted Date Caramel Sauce, then serve immediately.

Monkey Business

Makes one bowl

FOR THE BASE

¼ cup (60 ml) almond milk, plus more as needed

2½ frozen bananas

¼ tsp vanilla extract

Pinch of salt

FOR TOPPING

2 tbsp (30 ml) Honey Peanut Butter Drizzle (page 165)

2 tbsp (30 ml) Vegan Dark Chocolate Sauce (page 154)

3 Chocolate-Covered Frozen Banana Bites (page 171)

1 tbsp (3 g) puffed millet

Bananas are the base of so many smoothie bowls for a reason—they provide sweetness and creaminess as well as a rich, full-bodied texture. For this bowl, I'm putting bananas at the forefront, where they should be celebrated and loved just as much as monkeys love them. And what goes best with bananas? Chocolate and peanut butter (duh!).

I keep the Chocolate-Covered Frozen Banana Bites (page 171) in my freezer for a quick and easy, sweet, healthy snack. They make a great topping for this bowl (and others!).

Add the almond milk, frozen bananas, vanilla and salt to a blender or food processor. Blend on high, using a tamper tool to smash down the ingredients and help move things around. Stop to scrape down the sides every few minutes as needed. Blend until the mixture is nice and smooth, like ice cream. If needed, you can add more almond milk, 1 tablespoon (15 ml) at a time, to help move things along.

Transfer the mixture to a bowl, then swirl in the Honey Peanut Butter Drizzle and Vegan Dark Chocolate Sauce. Top with the Chocolate-Covered Frozen Banana Bites and puffed millet, then serve immediately.

Ingredient Spotlight: Puffed Millet.

This puffed grain cereal is a gluten-free, fat-free, high-in-fiber complete protein and tastes mildly earthy with a texture akin to popcorn. It adds a whimsical look to bowls, in addition to providing a slightly crunchy, pleasantly chewy texture. Look for it at health-food stores and online, or substitute any puffed grain or seed you can find.

Banana-Cream Pie

Makes one bowl

FOR THE BASE

¼ cup (60 ml) coconut milk, plus more as needed

½ tsp vanilla extract

2½ frozen bananas

2 tbsp (18 g) raw cashews, soaked overnight and drained

Pinch of salt

FOR TOPPING

¼ cup (38 g) Classic Granola (page 141)

½ banana, sliced

2 tbsp (30 ml) Coconut Whipped Cream (page 157)

Banana-cream pie is one of my all time favorite desserts, and luckily it translates GREAT into a smoothie bowl. This recipe is like eating a frozen slice, only this one is packed with nutrients and whole foods instead of cream and sugar. Frozen blended bananas and a few soaked cashews make up the rich, custardy base, while the Classic Granola (page 141) mimics the crunchy crust. I use Coconut Whipped Cream (page 157) to sub in for the real stuff, with fantastic results. If you're a banana-cream pie lover like me, this bowl has your name written all over it.

Add the coconut milk, vanilla, frozen bananas, cashews and salt to a blender or food processor. Blend on high, using a tamper tool, if available, to smash down the ingredients and stopping to scrape down the sides as needed. Blend until the mixture is smooth like ice cream, adding more coconut milk, 1 tablespoon (15 ml) at a time as needed, just to help it blend.

Transfer the mixture to a bowl, then sprinkle with the Classic Granola. Arrange the banana slices on top, then garnish with a dollop of Coconut Whipped Cream. Serve immediately.

Spicy Mexican Chocolate

Makes one bowl

FOR THE BASE

¼ cup (60 ml) coconut milk, plus more as needed

¼ tsp vanilla extract

2 frozen bananas

¼ avocado, peeled

1 tbsp (9 g) raw cacao powder or good-quality cocoa (see Ingredient Spotlight on page 154)

¼ tsp chili powder

¼ tsp cinnamon

Pinch of salt

FOR TOPPING

¼ cup (38 g) Chocolate Almond Granola (page 142)

2 tbsp (30 ml) Vegan Dark Chocolate Sauce (page 154)

Chili powder, for dusting

Inspired by Mexican hot chocolate, this bowl combines rich dark chocolate infused with a bit of cinnamon and spice. In ancient times, it's said that the Mayans enjoyed hot mugs of a rich chocolaty liquid that was flavored with various spices, and while it wasn't exactly a sweet drink, it eventually evolved into what we know as hot chocolate today.

Avocado provides extra creaminess, while chili powder gives just a bit of a spicy kick. Don't let that ingredient put you off, this bowl still tastes very mild; however, if you like it spicier, you can substitute some or all of the chili powder with cayenne pepper instead.

Add the coconut milk, vanilla, frozen bananas, avocado, cacao powder, chili powder, cinnamon and salt to a blender or food processor. Blend on high, using a tamper tool, if available, to smash down the ingredients, stopping to scrape down the sides as needed. Blend until the mixture is completely smooth. If the mixture is not blending well, you can add more coconut milk, 1 tablespoon (15 ml) at a time, to help move things along.

Transfer the mixture to a bowl, then sprinkle with the Chocolate Almond Granola. Drizzle with the Vegan Dark Chocolate Sauce, dust with the chili powder and serve immediately.

Cinnamon Pumpkin Pie

This bowl tastes like a frosty, frozen slice of pumpkin pie, only without the added sugar, gluten and dairy. It gets its sweetness from bananas and dates, and packs in a full half-cup (120 ml) of pumpkin purée. Cinnamon Pecan Granola (page 145) ties in even more fall flavor and adds a nice crunchy contrast to the smooth, creamy base. Call me basic, but this bowl makes all of my autumnal dreams come true.

FOR THE BASE

¼ cup (60 ml) almond milk, plus more as needed

¼ tsp pure vanilla extract

2 frozen bananas

½ cup (120 ml) unsweetened pumpkin purée

1 large date, soaked in hot water for 10 minutes, then drained

Pinch of sea salt

½ tsp pumpkin pie spice

FOR TOPPING

¼ cup (38 g) Cinnamon Pecan Granola (page 145)

2 tbsp (30 ml) Coconut Whipped Cream (page 157)

1 tbsp (9 g) shelled pumpkin seeds

Pumpkin pie spice, for dusting

Add the almond milk, vanilla, frozen bananas, pumpkin purée, date, salt and pumpkin pie spice to a blender or food processor. Blend on high, stopping to scrape down the sides every so often as needed. If available, use a tamper tool to smash down the ingredients and help facilitate blending. Add more almond milk, 1 tablespoon (15 ml) at a time as needed, just to get everything moving.

Transfer the mixture to a bowl, then sprinkle with the Cinnamon Pecan Granola. Top with the Coconut Whipped Cream, sprinkle with the pumpkin seeds, dust with the pumpkin pie spice and serve immediately.

Toasted Coconut Caramel

Makes one bowl

FOR THE TOASTED COCONUT TOPPING

2 tbsp (10 g) unsweetened wide coconut flakes, shavings or "chips"

FOR THE BASE

¼ cup (60 ml) coconut milk, plus more as needed

¼ tsp vanilla extract

4 (1-oz [30-ml]) coconut milk ice cubes (see tutorial on page 9)

2 frozen bananas

2 tbsp (30 g) coconut butter

Pinch of sea salt

FOR TOPPING

2 tbsp (30 ml) Coconut Whipped Cream (page 157)

2 tbsp (30 ml) Salted Date Caramel Sauce (page 158)

Tip: Coconut flakes come in all different shapes and sizes. This recipe works best with large, wide flakes, which are sometimes labeled as "chips" or "shavings."

It's no secret that I'm a huge fan of coconut. Most of the recipes in this book call for plain dried coconut flakes, but this recipe switches it up with toasted coconut instead. Toasting coconut, just like with most nuts, brings out a deeper, richer flavor that pairs magically with caramel.

This recipe calls for coconut in five different forms—coconut milk ice cubes, coconut butter, coconut milk, coconut flakes and Coconut Whipped Cream (page 157)—so if you love coconut, let this be the first bowl you make. Salted Date Caramel Sauce (page 158) gilds the lily by providing a salty-sweet contrast to the smooth, creamy coconut.

Preheat the oven to 350°F (180°C). Place the coconut flakes on a dry sheet pan, and bake for about 10 minutes, or until lightly toasted. Toss them once about halfway through the cook time to promote even browning, and keep an eye on them so they don't burn. Let cool completely, then set aside.

Add the coconut milk, vanilla, coconut milk ice cubes, frozen bananas, coconut butter and salt to a blender or food processor. Blend on high, stopping to scrape down the sides every so often as needed. If you have a tamper tool available, use it to smash down the ingredients and move things around. Blend until smooth, adding more coconut milk, 1 tablespoon (15 ml) at a time as needed, just to get everything moving.

Transfer the mixture to a bowl, dollop with the Coconut Whipped Cream, drizzle with the Salted Date Caramel Sauce, then sprinkle with the toasted coconut flakes. Serve immediately.

Black & White Cookie

Inspired by the classic New York City black & white cookie, this smoothie bowl is just as satisfying but packs in so much more nutrition. This smoothie bowl mixes chocolate and vanilla for a modern-looking bowl that's as fun to make as it is to eat. Black sesame seeds and white coconut flakes further heighten the contrasting colors.

FOR THE BASE

¼ cup (60 ml) coconut milk, plus more as needed

¼ tsp vanilla extract

4 (1-oz [30-ml]) coconut milk ice cubes (see tutorial on page 9)

2 frozen bananas

Pinch of sea salt

1 tbsp (15 ml) honey

1 tbsp (9 g) cocoa powder

½ tsp activated charcoal powder (see Ingredient Spotlight on page 58)

FOR TOPPING

1 tbsp (9 g) unsweetened coconut flakes

2 tsp (6 g) black sesame seeds

Add the coconut milk, vanilla, coconut milk ice cubes, frozen bananas, salt and honey to a blender or food processor. Blend on high, using a tamper tool, if available, to smash down the ingredients and stopping to scrape down the sides as needed. Blend until the mixture is as smooth as ice cream, adding more coconut milk, 1 tablespoon (15 ml) at a time as needed to get everything moving. Try to use as little liquid as possible in order to keep it nice and thick.

Transfer half of the mixture to one side of a bowl, then immediately place the bowl in the freezer. Blend or hand mix the remaining mixture with the cocoa powder and activated charcoal until it's evenly dark in color. Remove the bowl from the freezer, then place the remaining mixture on the other side of the bowl, being careful to keep an even line of separation in the center. Sprinkle the white half with coconut flakes, and the black half with black sesame seeds. Serve immediately.

Pro Styling Tip: For a super clean edge for your toppings, hold a piece of cardboard or stiff paper directly over the side you don't wish to cover, then sprinkle the exposed side with toppings. This will help keep the line straight.

Tip: Activated charcoal is a relatively harmless ingredient, but it can interact with certain medications. If you're not sure, consult a health-care practitioner before using.

Cherry Cheesecake

Makes one bowl

FOR THE BASE

¼ cup (60 ml) coconut milk, plus more as needed

2 tsp (10 ml) lemon juice

½ tsp vanilla extract

2 (1-oz [30-ml]) coconut milk ice cubes (see tutorial on page 9)

2 frozen bananas

¼ cup (38 g) frozen pitted cherries

Pinch of sea salt

2 tbsp (18 g) raw cashews, soaked overnight and drained

FOR TOPPING

¼ cup (38 g) Classic Granola (page 141)

3–4 fresh cherries (whole or pitted and sliced)

This bowl tastes just like a frozen cherry cheesecake. A combination of bananas, coconut milk ice cubes and soaked raw cashews are blended up to create an incredibly creamy base that gets a hint of tang from both the cherries and a spritz of fresh lemon juice. Because the base of this recipe is so flavorful on its own, I keep the topping fairly simple. A little bit of Classic Granola (page 141) mimics the graham cracker crust of a classic New York–style cheesecake while providing a nice crunchy texture to contrast the cool, smooth filling. You can add pitted sliced cherries to the top if you wish, but I'm too lazy to bother with pitting them and find that a few whole cherries for garnish is all it needs.

Add the coconut milk, lemon juice, vanilla, coconut milk ice cubes, frozen bananas, frozen cherries, salt and cashews to a blender or food processor. Blend on high until nice and smooth. Use a tamper tool, if available, to smash down the ingredients and stop to scrape down the sides as needed. Add more coconut milk, 1 tablespoon (15 ml) at a time, to help facilitate blending if needed.

Transfer the mixture to a bowl, then sprinkle with the Classic Granola. Top with the cherries and serve immediately.

Tip: Look for frozen pitted cherries in the frozen-fruit section of your grocery store. Freezing them yourself is always an option, but you'll have to painstakingly pit each one.

Toppings Are
Everything

◀▲▶

Toppings make the bowl, and I often consider them the best part. This chapter gets creative with all kinds of different ways to top your bowls. You don't have to stick to the classic granola, fruit and honey routine. You can go crazy with just about anything your brain can conjure up. Think outside of the box and have fun. Take risks and try something new, or keep it simple, if that's what you prefer. Regardless of which toppings are called for on a particular bowl, you always have the option to add or remove different items as you see fit.

In addition to several granola recipes, you'll find healthier versions of your favorite ice cream toppings, like the Vegan Dark Chocolate Sauce (page 154), as well as a few clever nut and seed blends that will up the nutritional profile of your bowls in a serious way. There's even a fun tutorial for making the frilly Dried Pineapple Flowers (page 167) that are typically used as a cake decoration, but look just as good, if not better, perched on top of a smoothie bowl.

Adding a slew of diversely textured and interesting toppings to a bowl makes it so much more fun and interesting to eat, which is why I had to create an entire chapter on the subject. The following recipes all make great additions to the bowls in this book, but most of them are excellent stand-alone recipes as well.

Classic Granola

Makes about
1½ quarts (1.6 kg)

4 cups (360 g) old-fashioned rolled oats

1 cup (50 g) unsweetened large coconut flakes

½ cup (65 g) sunflower seeds

⅓ cup (67 g) coconut sugar or brown sugar (see Ingredient Spotlight on page 145)

1 tsp kosher salt

⅓ cup (80 ml) maple syrup or honey

⅓ cup (80 ml) melted coconut, canola or grapeseed oil

This is the recipe we've become known for at Soulberri because it's what we use to top all of our famous "Soul Bowls." It's gluten free and totally vegan, making it something everyone can enjoy. This is a versatile, everyday granola that tastes great on just about any bowl and is practically impossible to mess up. This recipe is pretty perfect as-is, but it takes extremely well to customizations.

Preheat the oven to 300°F (150°C) and line a sheet pan with parchment paper.

In a large bowl, mix together the oats, coconut flakes, sunflower seeds, coconut sugar and salt. Pour the maple syrup and oil over the oat mixture, then toss until every piece is thoroughly coated.

Spread the granola onto the sheet pan in an even layer, then bake until golden brown and toasted, about 45 minutes to 1 hour. About halfway through the cooking time, use a spatula to gently stir everything around to promote even cooking.

Allow the granola to cool completely, then crumble into pieces. Keep the granola in an airtight container at room temperature for up to 3 weeks.

Ingredient Spotlight: Oats.
This humble grain is technically gluten free; however, if you're trying to completely avoid gluten it's important to source a brand that is certified gluten free. This is because oats are typically processed in a facility that also processes gluten-containing wheat products, which poses the risk of cross-contamination. Certified gluten-free oats are guaranteed to be void of all gluten and therefore pose no risk to those with extreme sensitivity.

Chocolate Almond Granola

Makes about
1½ quarts (1.6 kg)

3 cups (270 g) rolled oats (see Ingredient Spotlight on page 141)

1 cup (50 g) unsweetened large coconut flakes

1 cup (130 g) sliced or slivered almonds

⅓ cup (50 g) coconut sugar (see Ingredient Spotlight on page 145)

3 tbsp (24 g) raw cacao powder or good-quality cocoa powder (see Ingredient Spotlight on page 154)

1 tsp kosher salt

⅓ cup (80 ml) agave nectar, honey or maple syrup

⅓ cup (80 ml) melted coconut, grapeseed or canola oil

Sure, this recipe is packed with nutrient-dense ingredients like oats, almonds and cacao, but it tastes like a crunchy chocolate oatmeal cookie. It's just sweet enough, intensely chocolaty and has a decent amount of salt to balance out the flavors. Not only does this add a satisfying chocolate crunch to many of the bowls in this book (like the Cookies & Cream bowl on page 114), it's just as tasty in a bowl with milk.

Preheat the oven to 300°F (150°C) and line a sheet pan with parchment paper.

In a large bowl, mix together the oats, coconut flakes, almonds, coconut sugar, cacao powder and salt.

Pour the agave nectar and oil over the oat mixture and toss until every piece is thoroughly coated.

Spread the granola onto the sheet pan in an even layer, then bake until toasted, about 45 minutes to 1 hour. Use a spatula to gently stir everything around halfway through the cooking time to promote even cooking. Because the granola is already dark from the cacao powder, you won't be able to tell from the color alone that it is done. So, at about 45 minutes of cook time, taste a piece; it should be crunchy and lightly toasted, not soft, raw or burnt.

Allow the granola to cool completely, then crumble into pieces. Keep in an airtight container at room temperature for up to 3 weeks.

Cinnamon Pecan Granola

Makes about
1½ quarts (1.6 kg)

3 cups (270 g) rolled oats (see Ingredient Spotlight on page 141)

1 cup (50 g) unsweetened large coconut flakes

1 cup (130 g) chopped pecans

⅓ cup (50 g) coconut sugar or dark brown sugar

1 tsp cinnamon

½ tsp ginger

¼ tsp nutmeg

¾ tsp kosher salt

⅓ cup (80 ml) maple syrup, honey or agave nectar

⅓ cup (80 ml) melted coconut, grapeseed or canola oil

If you're craving a warm piece of apple crisp or blueberry crumble pie, this is the recipe for you. It's the granola I reach for any time I'm making a smoothie bowl that would benefit from a little bit of cinnamon and spice, like the Cinnamon Pumpkin Pie bowl (page 130). The warm spices add an incredible boost of flavor in addition to some added nutrition. Cinnamon is high in antioxidants and is a natural anti-inflammatory, so this granola will leave you feeling as good as it tastes.

Preheat the oven to 300°F (150°C) and line a sheet pan with parchment paper.

In a large bowl, mix together the oats, coconut flakes, pecans, coconut sugar, cinnamon, ginger, nutmeg and salt. Pour the maple syrup and oil over the oat mixture and toss until every piece is thoroughly coated.

Spread the granola onto the sheet pan, then bake until toasted, about 45 minutes to 1 hour. About halfway through the cooking time, use a spatula to gently stir everything around to promote even cooking.

Allow the granola to cool completely, then crumble into pieces. Keep in an airtight container at room temperature for up to 3 weeks.

Ingredient Spotlight: Coconut Sugar.

This dark, granulated sweetener is extracted from the nectar of coconut flowers, and has a slightly earthy, caramel flavor. Because it's unrefined and has a low glycemic index, this sweetener has been touted as a healthy alternative to table sugar. Look for it at health-food stores and online, or substitute date sugar, evaporated cane juice, turbanado, raw sugar or light brown sugar instead.

Super Seed Granola

2 cups (180 g) rolled oats (see Ingredient Spotlight on page 141)

1 cup (50 g) unsweetened large coconut flakes

½ cup (65 g) shelled sunflower seeds

½ cup (65 g) shelled pumpkin seeds

¼ cup (50 g) raw millet

¼ cup (50 g) raw quinoa

¼ cup (50 g) raw buckwheat groats

2 tbsp (18 g) chia seeds

2 tbsp (18 g) flaxseed meal or ground flaxseed

¼ cup (36 g) hemp seeds (see Ingredient Spotlight on page 77)

2 tbsp (18 g) sesame seeds

⅓ cup (50 g) coconut sugar (see Ingredient Spotlight on page 145)

1 tsp kosher salt

⅓ cup (80 ml) maple syrup, agave nectar or honey

⅓ cup (80 ml) melted coconut, canola or grapeseed oil

This specialty granola is jam-packed with so many nutrient-dense seeds. Many people think of millet, quinoa and buckwheat as being grains since they're commonly prepared that way, but they're all technically seeds, and seriously healthy ones at that. They're loaded with fiber, protein and numerous vitamins and minerals.

This blend tastes similar to the Classic Granola (page 141), only it includes far more nutrients. This is the healthiest granola recipe in this book because it's loaded with all kinds of superfoods like quinoa, chia seeds, flaxseed and hemp seeds. Swap this recipe out for any other granola on your favorite bowl for long-lasting energy.

Preheat the oven to 300°F (150°C) and line a sheet pan with parchment paper.

In a large bowl, mix together the oats, coconut flakes, sunflower seeds, pumpkin seeds, millet, quinoa, buckwheat groats, chia seeds, flaxseed meal, hemp seeds, sesame seeds, coconut sugar and salt. Pour the maple syrup and oil over the oat mixture and toss until every piece is thoroughly coated.

Spread the mixture onto the sheet pan, then bake until toasted, about 45 minutes to 1 hour. About halfway through the cooking time, use a spatula to gently stir everything around to promote even cooking.

Allow the granola to cool completely, then crumble into pieces. Keep in an airtight container at room temperature for up to 3 weeks.

Power Seed Sprinkle

Makes about ½ cup
(65 g)

2 tbsp (18 g) hemp seeds (see
Ingredient Spotlight on page 77)

2 tbsp (18 g) flaxseed meal or
ground flaxseed

1 tbsp (9 g) sunflower seeds

1 tbsp (12 g) sesame seeds

1 tbsp (10 g) chia seeds

This powerhouse topping packs in a crazy amount of nutrition. Each seed is loaded with its own arsenal of micronutrients, antioxidants, protein, fiber, vitamins and minerals. This topping also adds amazing crunch and textural contrast to bowls. I like to make big batches of it and keep it in the freezer for longer storage and to maximize freshness.

Mix together the hemp seeds, flaxseed meal, sunflower seeds, sesame seeds and chia seeds in a small bowl, then transfer the mixture to an airtight container. Store at room temperature for up to 3 weeks, or in the freezer for 6 months or longer.

Bird Seed Brittle

¼ cup (50 g) raw quinoa

¼ cup (50 g) raw millet

¾ cup (75 g) finely shredded coconut flakes

¼ cup (33 g) shelled pumpkin seeds

2 tbsp (25 g) sesame seeds

¼ cup (38 g) coconut sugar (see Ingredient Spotlight on page 145)

¼ tsp sea salt, plus more for topping

2 tbsp (30 ml) coconut oil

⅓ cup (80 ml) honey or maple syrup

This recipe is a healthier version of a peanut brittle. It's made with tons of superfoods, which are loaded with protein, fiber and healthy fats. The recipe bakes up to be a crunchy, salty-sweet treat, and I'm willing to bet the birds would love it (almost) as much as you will.

Preheat the oven to 300°F (150°C) and line a sheet pan with parchment paper.

Combine the quinoa, millet, coconut, pumpkin seeds, sesame seeds, coconut sugar and salt in a medium bowl. Add the coconut oil and honey to a small saucepan over medium-low heat. Stir until the coconut oil has melted, then pour over the seed mixture and stir until every piece is thoroughly coated.

Transfer the mixture to the prepared baking sheet, then use a rubber spatula to spread it out into an even layer. Try to get it as even as possible so that it cooks consistently throughout. It's okay if small holes form, they will fill in as it cooks. Make a clean edge around the perimeter.

Bake for 25 to 30 minutes, rotating the pan once, about halfway through the cooking time. Keep an eye on it throughout cooking to make sure the edges don't burn. It's done when it turns a deep caramel color throughout and smells nutty and fragrant.

Allow the brittle to cool completely before breaking it into bite-size pieces. Store the brittle in a tightly sealed container for a few days at room temperature or up to 3 months in the freezer. I prefer to keep it in the freezer because it can get a bit soggy at room temperature, especially when it's humid. Plus, the frozen bits taste especially good atop a smoothie bowl!

Sweet Dukkah

Makes about 1 cup (150 g)

¼ cup (40 g) whole almonds

¼ cup (40 g) whole pistachios (shelled)

¼ cup (50 g) sesame seeds

1 tbsp (10 g) coconut sugar (see Ingredient Spotlight on page 145)

¼ tsp flaky sea salt

½ tsp ground coriander

½ tsp ground cinnamon

¼ tsp ground cardamom

1 tbsp (6 g) grated orange zest

1 tbsp (3 g) crumbled dried rose petals (optional)

Dukkah is an Egyptian spice mix that's typically mixed with olive oil and served as a dip for pita bread. It's been gaining traction recently in the culinary world, with chefs using it to top everything from avocado toast to grilled meats and fish. I created a sweet version with warm spices like cinnamon and cardamom so it's perfectly suited for smoothie bowls.

Dukkah means "to pound" in Arabic, which refers to the method used to grind the nuts, seeds and spices into a roughly textured mix. This recipe makes more than enough for a smoothie bowl, but it will keep fresh for up to a month stored in an airtight container, and even longer in the freezer.

Heat a medium skillet over medium heat. Add the almonds and cook, stirring constantly, for 3 to 4 minutes, then add the pistachios and cook until they're lightly toasted, 2 to 3 minutes more. Transfer the nuts to the bowl of a mortar and pestle, then add the sesame seeds to the pan. Cook the sesame seeds, stirring constantly, until lightly toasted, about 2 minutes. Add the sesame seeds to the mortar and pestle, then pulverize until the almonds and pistachios are broken into small bits.

Add the coconut sugar, salt, coriander, cinnamon, cardamom, orange zest and rose petals (if using), then continue pounding until you reach your desired texture. You can leave it fairly coarse or more powdery if you prefer. Transfer the mixture to an airtight container and store in a cool, dry place for up to 1 month, or up to 6 months in the freezer.

Vegan Dark Chocolate Sauce

Makes about 1 pint (0.5 L)

1 (14-oz [400-g]) can coconut cream

⅓ cup (50 g) coconut sugar (see Ingredient Spotlight on page 145)

½ cup (64 g) raw cacao powder or good-quality cocoa powder

1½ tsp (8 ml) vanilla extract

¼ tsp flaky sea salt

Made with coconut cream, unrefined coconut sugar and antioxidant-rich cacao powder, this ultra chocolaty dessert condiment is surprisingly healthy, even though it tastes downright sinful. Because of the coconut milk, it doesn't keep for more than a few days in the fridge, but I found that if you freeze it and reheat it gently, it comes back to life as good as it was the first day you made it.

Combine the coconut cream, coconut sugar and cacao powder in a medium saucepan over medium-low heat. Bring up to a gentle simmer and continuously whisk until smooth, 5 to 8 minutes. Remove from the heat, then stir in the vanilla and sea salt. Let cool.

Transfer the sauce to a jar or resealable container, then place a piece of plastic wrap on top of the sauce and press it down so it makes contact. This will prevent it from forming a skin, like pudding. Store the sauce in the refrigerator for about 5 days, or freeze for longer storage. Warm slightly and stir before using.

Tip: If coconut cream is unavailable, you can substitute a can of full-fat (not light) coconut milk along with 1 tablespoon (15 ml) of coconut oil (without the oil it will be too thin).

Ingredient Spotlight: Cocoa/Cacao Powder.

Cacao is the antioxidant-rich plant that is used to make chocolate, and in its raw form can taste bitter and acidic. Cocoa is cacao that's been roasted to make it sweeter and more palatable, but many of the naturally occurring nutrients are destroyed in the process. Cocoa and cacao can be used interchangeably in the recipes in this book, but the flavor and nutritional benefits will vary.

Coconut Whipped Cream

Makes about 1 cup (240 ml)

1 (14-oz [400-g]) can unsweetened full-fat coconut milk

½ tsp vanilla extract

1 tbsp (15 ml) honey, agave nectar or maple syrup, more or less to taste

Pinch of salt

Tip: It's very important to use a brand of coconut milk that doesn't contain any added stabilizers like guar gum, which will prevent the coconut cream from separating, making it impossible to whip. Trader Joe's organic coconut milk whips up very well, in addition to the Thai brand Arroy-D. Whole Foods 365 organic full-fat coconut milk is the only brand I've found that whips up nicely even though it still contains a stabilizer.

This recipe holds the power to turn any smoothie bowl into a bona fide dessert. It's the literal icing on the cake! Coconut Whipped Cream is made almost exactly like traditional whipped cream, and has a mellow, but delicious coconut flavor, making it an awesome replacement for the real thing.

Refrigerate the can of coconut milk for at least 2 hours, and up to 12, but no more than that. (Sometimes when the coconut milk becomes too cold and separated, the resulting whipped cream will be grainy and difficult to whip.) Without shaking the can, open it up and use a spoon to scoop out the thick layer of cream that's floating on top. Discard the watery liquid left behind, or save it for later use in a smoothie (freeze for longer storage).

Add the cream to a medium bowl. Using an electric mixer, whip the coconut cream until it becomes aerated and thick. You can also do this by hand with a whisk, it will just take a little bit longer. Add the vanilla, as much or as little of whichever sweetener you prefer and the salt. One tablespoon (15 ml) of sweetener will result in a barely sweet whipped cream, so if you prefer it sweeter feel free to add more. You can also leave the sweetener out completely for an unsweetened cream.

Store leftover coconut cream refrigerated in an airtight container for up to 5 days.

Salted Date Caramel Sauce

Makes about 1 ½ pints (0.7 L)

2 cups (300 g) pitted dates, packed

Boiling water

⅔ cup (160 ml) full-fat coconut milk or cream

2 tsp (10 ml) vanilla extract

1 tsp flaky sea salt

The first time I tried making a caramel sauce out of dates I was blown away at how close it tasted to the real thing. Dates have a naturally caramel flavor, making them the perfect ingredient to use as the base for this recipe. Soaking them first in boiling water allows them to become completely soft so that they blend up nice and smooth. Coconut milk adds creaminess, while a hefty dose of salt counters the date's natural sweetness, making this an irresistible topping for practically any smoothie bowl.

Add the dates to a medium bowl, then cover them with boiling water. Let them soak for at least an hour, or longer if you have the time. The softer they get, the better. Drain the dates, but reserve the soaking liquid.

Add the dates to a blender along with the coconut milk, vanilla and salt. Blend on high until completely smooth, adding reserved soaking liquid a little bit at a time until you reach your desired consistency. You can keep it relatively thick or on the thinner side. I like it to be about the consistency of pancake batter. The total amount of added water will depend on the moisture content of your dates as well as your personal preference.

Transfer the sauce to a jar or squeeze bottle and refrigerate for up to a week. For longer storage, keep the sauce in the freezer and defrost and reblend if needed before using.

Chocolate Hazelnut Butter

Makes about 1 pint (0.5 L)

2 cups (130 g) raw hazelnuts

2 tbsp (16 g) raw cacao powder or good-quality cocoa powder (see Ingredient Spotlight on page 154)

½ cup (75 g) coconut sugar (see Ingredient Spotlight on page 145)

¾ cup (180 ml) full-fat coconut milk, plus more as needed

1 tsp vanilla extract

¾ tsp sea salt

Tip: If you can find skinned hazelnuts, they will be best for this recipe as they won't require the tedious process of removing the skins after roasting. If you're using pre-roasted hazelnuts, it's still beneficial to throw them in the oven for 5 to 8 minutes because they'll blend easier when they are hot.

This recipe is a homemade, completely vegan version of the popular chocolate hazelnut spread Nutella. It's not only healthier because it's void of refined sugar, dairy and preservatives, it also has a more pronounced chocolate-hazelnut flavor. This stuff is perfect for topping the more dessert-worthy smoothie bowls, especially the Chocolate Hazelnut bowl (page 118), but it's also pretty darn good eaten by the spoonful right out of the jar! Not that I know from experience or anything . . . Just try not to polish off the entire batch in one sitting.

Preheat the oven to 350°F (180°C).

Place the hazelnuts on a sheet pan and roast for 10 to 15 minutes or until they smell nutty and appear lightly browned. If using skin-on nuts, transfer them to a damp kitchen towel, then vigorously rub to remove as much of the skins as possible (it may be difficult to get them off completely, but do the best you can). Discard the skins and place the nuts in a blender or food processor.

Blend on high until the nuts form a smooth paste (this may take 5 minutes or longer depending on your machine), then add the cacao powder, coconut sugar, coconut milk, vanilla and salt. If the mixture is very thick or if separation occurs, add more coconut milk, 1 tablespoon (15 ml) at a time, while blending until the mixture is totally smooth.

Transfer the mixture to a jar, then keep refrigerated for up to a month or in the freezer for longer storage.

Magic Toppings

CHOCOLATE MAGIC

¾ cup (96 g) raw cacao or
good-quality cocoa powder (see
Ingredient Spotlight on page
154)

1½ cups (360 ml) melted
coconut oil

¼ cup (60 ml) agave nectar,
maple syrup or honey

NUT/SEED BUTTER MAGIC

1 cup (240 ml) melted coconut
oil

1 cup (250 g) peanut butter,
almond butter, cashew butter,
sunflower butter or your favorite
nut butter

COCONUT MAGIC

2 cups (480 ml) melted coconut
oil

½ cup (35 g) finely shredded
coconut flakes

These are some of our most popular bowl toppings at Soulberri.
They're a homemade, healthier version of the classic ice-cream
topping known as "Magic Shell." They each have a coconut-
oil base that causes them to immediately harden upon contact
with anything cold—like a smoothie bowl. The hardened topping
is crunchy at first, but melts the instant it hits your tongue. I've
included the ingredients for three different varieties—chocolate,
nut/seed butter and coconut—but the directions are the same for
each. Feel free to play around and add different flavorings to
create a unique topping that's all your own.

Select which kind of magic you'd like to make, then whisk together all
the ingredients for that variety until smooth. Transfer the topping to a jar
or squeeze bottle, then store at room temperature for up to a month.
Separation will occur over time, so shake or stir well before every use. If
the coconut oil hardens, gently heat in the microwave for a few seconds
or in a warm water bath until it melts, then whisk to recombine.

Nut & Seed Butter Drizzles

Makes about ½ cup (120 ml) each

HONEY PEANUT BUTTER DRIZZLE

⅓ cup (85 g) peanut butter (raw or roasted)

1 tbsp (15 ml) honey, or more or less to taste

3 tbsp (45 ml) warm water, plus more as needed

VANILLA CASHEW BUTTER DRIZZLE

⅓ cup (85 g) cashew butter (raw or roasted)

1 tbsp (15 ml) agave nectar, or more or less to taste

2 tsp (10 ml) vanilla extract

3 tbsp (45 ml) warm water, plus more as needed

Peanut butter, almond butter, chocolate hazelnut butter, cashew butter and really any nut or seed butter is an excellent topping for smoothie bowls. A big scoop of nut butter works in a pinch, but I like them better when they're a bit more liquified and can be drizzled on top of or swirled into the bowl instead. These nut and seed butter drizzles are lightly sweetened and loosened up with a bit of water to make them ideal for drizzling, swirling and eating. There are endless flavor combinations you can make; these are just some of my favorites. Feel free to experiment with different pairings and have fun creating new flavors.

For all of the recipes, add the nut/seed butter, sweeteners and any flavorings to a small bowl. Whisk in the warm water, adding more if needed to reach a consistency that can be drizzled. The total amount of water you will need will depend on the thickness of your nut/seed butter.

(continued)

Nut & Seed Butter Drizzles (Continued)

CHOCOLATE HAZELNUT DRIZZLE

⅓ cup (80 ml) Chocolate Hazelnut Butter (page 161, or store-bought)

3 tbsp (45 ml) warm water, plus more as needed

CINNAMON ALMOND BUTTER DRIZZLE

⅓ cup (80 ml) almond butter (raw or roasted)

1 tbsp (15 ml) agave nectar, or more or less to taste

1 tsp cinnamon

3 tbsp (45 ml) warm water, plus more as needed

TAHINI MAPLE DRIZZLE

⅓ cup (80 ml) raw tahini

2 tbsp (30 ml) maple syrup, or more or less to taste

Pinch of salt

3 tbsp (45 ml) warm water, plus more as needed

Store the drizzles in an airtight container in the refrigerator for up to 1 week. Bring to room temperature and stir to loosen before using.

Tip: If your nut/seed butter is unsalted, you may want to add a pinch of salt to bring out the flavors.

Dried Pineapple Flowers

Makes about
25 flowers (amount
will vary depending
on the size of your
pineapple)

1 whole fresh pineapple

These frilly, pale yellow flowers aren't actually flowers at all; they're made from dried slices of pineapple.

While Dried Pineapple Flowers may seem like a fussy addition to a simple smoothie bowl, there's no doubt they make eating one a lot more fun. Making them is actually an easy process, it just takes a bit of time for the pineapple slices to dry out. They don't keep for very long at room temperature, especially during humid weather, so I like to keep them in the freezer instead.

Cut the top and bottom off of the pineapple, then run your knife down the sides to remove the rind. Use a small melon baller or measuring spoon to cut out the "eyes" and any pieces of skin that remain. The holes will create a beautiful frilly edge once the pineapple flowers are finished, so don't be shy about digging into the pineapple.

Preheat the oven to 200°F (95°C) and line two sheet pans with parchment paper (or more if needed).

Thinly slice the pineapple into rounds about ⅛ inch (3 mm) thick. Take your time and be sure to make the slices as even as possible.

(continued)

Dried Pineapple Flowers (Continued)

Lay the pineapple slices on the parchment-lined sheet pans in an even layer, then use a paper towel to blot off some of their moisture—this will help them dry out faster.

Bake for approximately 2 hours, rotating the pans every 30 minutes or so. You want the flowers to be dried out, firm to the touch and just a little bit darker around the edges, but not browned. This may happen sooner than 2 hours, or it may take longer. The time will ultimately depend on your oven as well as the thickness and moisture content of your pineapple. The pieces on the outside may be done before the ones in the center, so remove them while the others continue cooking.

Allow the flowers to cool completely, then transfer them to an airtight container. They can be stored at room temperature for about a day or so, but any longer and they will get soft. If it's particularly humid in your house, it may take even less than a day for them to soften. I like to store them in the freezer, but be aware that freezing will make them very brittle. Make sure they are in a hard container and not a bag, otherwise they can easily be crushed.

Use pineapple flowers to garnish your favorite smoothie bowls.

Chocolate-Covered Frozen Banana Bites

Makes 16 to
22 pieces,
depending on size

2 ripe bananas (yellow with few brown spots, if any)

⅓ cup (85 g) raw cacao or good-quality cocoa powder (see Ingredient Spotlight on page 154)

⅔ cup (160 ml) melted coconut oil, cooled

1 tbsp (15 ml) agave nectar, maple syrup or honey

Tip: The chocolate mixture used in this recipe is just a condensed recipe for the Chocolate Magic (page 162). I recommend making the full amount of Chocolate Magic and keeping the rest on hand as a fun smoothie bowl topping.

These little frozen nuggets of chocolaty goodness are one of my favorite healthy snacks to keep on hand, and they make an awesome topping for smoothie bowls too. They're super simple to make and will keep in the freezer for months, so they're perfect for a quick chocolate fix. When added to a smoothie bowl, they add textural contrast and visual interest as well.

Line a sheet pan with parchment paper.

Slice the bananas ½ inch (13 mm) thick, then place them on the sheet pan in an even layer. Freeze until solid, at least 4 to 6 hours.

Whisk together the cacao powder, melted coconut oil and agave nectar until smooth.

Remove the sheet pan from the freezer, then use a fork to dip a banana slice into the chocolate mixture, being sure to coat it on all sides. Allow any excess to drip off, then carefully transfer the banana slice back to the parchment-lined sheet pan. Repeat with the remaining banana slices. If the chocolate mixture seizes up during the process, place it in the microwave or warm it over a double boiler for a few seconds, or until melted, but not hot.

Return the sheet pan to the freezer and allow the chocolate to firm up, about 30 minutes. Transfer the banana slices to an airtight container and keep them in the freezer for up to 3 months.

Acknowledgments

Thank you to all my friends and family for your honesty, your ideas and especially your patience when I was a little crazier (okay, a lot crazier) than normal as I worked through this project. An extra-special thank you goes to my husband and my dad—I could not have written this book without your continued love and support.

Thank you to Emma Frisch, Loreal Gavin, Samantha Ferraro and Jessie Johnson for your priceless advice, guidance and words of encouragement. Thank you to Zina and Don Brown for sharing your gorgeous handmade pottery that became the homes for so many of the smoothie bowls pictured in this book.

Thank you to Rebecca Fofonoff and the entire team at Page Street Publishing for believing in me and my ideas, as well as all the guidance and support provided throughout the book-writing process.

Thank you to my puppy Phoebe for keeping me company and providing comic relief during the long hours spent writing and recipe testing, and for eating all the bananas I dropped on the floor.

And finally, a huge thank you to Chaser, Will, Ryan and the entire "Soul Squad" at Soulberri for your hard work, dedication and endless inspiration.

About the Author

Nicole Gaffney, aka Coley, is a professionally trained chef, recipe developer, food writer and TV personality best known for being second runner up on season 10 of *Food Network Star*. She's also a co-owner of Soulberri Smoothies and Bowls, located in her hometown of Brigantine, New Jersey.

Nicole draws most of her inspiration from the land and the sea. She makes her home at the Jersey shore and is both an avid gardener and farmers' market groupie. Nicole is passionate about sustainability and believes that quality ingredients are the key to making simple food taste great.

Nicole is host of the long-running syndicated cooking TV show, *The Chef's Kitchen*, and makes regular appearances on QVC. She's also been featured on *The Today Show*, *The Rachael Ray Show*, *House Hunters* and *My Family Recipe Rocks*. Nicole is a regular contributor to *Flavor Magazine*, The Daily Meal and Honest Cooking, and has been featured in *Food Network Magazine*, *Serendipity* magazine and *Spoonful* magazine.

Nicole's blog, ColeyCooks.com, is home to hundreds of recipes, cooking tutorials and instructional videos.

Index